Pra

MW00529820

Peaceful Discipline

Story Teaching, Brain Science & Better Behavior

"Offering a balance of science, practical experience, and new perspectives, *Peaceful Discipline* guides parents to a lifetime of easier, deeper, and stronger relationships with their kids."

—Tina Payne Bryson, PhD, *New York Times* best-selling author of *The Whole-Brain Child* and *No-Drama Discipline*

"Accessible, tender, and wise, this book provides parents with actionable tips and strategies that will forge more connected and joyful relationships!"

—Mona Delahooke, PhD, best-selling author of *Beyond Behaviors* and *Brain-Body Parenting*

"I really enjoyed *Peaceful Discipline*. Families can immediately benefit from trying these ideas, many of which don't appear in other parenting books. I particularly liked the storytelling angle. This book is a straightforward and encouraging recipe for a more peaceful life with children."

—Jessica Joelle Alexander, best-selling coauthor of *The Danish Way of Parenting*

"In a world filled with seemingly contradictory, overly complicated, highlight-reel parenting advice, Sarah Moore offers a refreshingly honest, research-backed, joyful approach to raising our children in ways that best support them and us. Her focus on the parent-child relationship, brain development, and emotional regulation provides a foundation for the many practical concepts and strategies she provides. This book is a must-read for parents raising kids of all ages and will benefit those with neurotypical, as well as neurodivergent, children. I look forward to recommending it widely at my clinic and beyond."

—Nicole Beurkens, PhD, licensed psychologist

"Sarah consistently reminds us that there's no such thing as a perfect parent. We are all on our own learning path. There's definitely no judgment in this book! Just solid support and advice. It's the practical, everyday life examples that really stood out for me. Sarah looks at peaceful, playful ways to resolve common struggles."

—Vivek Patel, *Meaningful Ideas*

"I know Sarah personally and she's the real deal. *Peaceful Discipline* is a gift to parents everywhere. It's practical, insightful, and funny. It gives us tools we can use in the moment, as well as to lay the foundation for a lifetime of connection with our kids. Sarah covers not only *what* to do but *why*. I highly recommend it for every home where children live."

—Michele Borba, EdD, author of *Thrivers: The Surprising Reasons Why Some Kids Struggle and Others Shine*

"Sarah R. Moore is the godmother of peaceful discipline! In *Peaceful Discipline*, Sarah has crafted an essential guide for every parent. It charts a path for parents to experience the joy of parenting. 'Story teaching' is a truly wonderful way of helping children gain the needed skills for a lifetime of happiness. I thought I knew just about every idea and strategy for parenting, but Sarah reminded me of how much more I could learn."

—Sam Goldstein, PhD, coauthor of *Tenacity in Children*
adjunct assistant professor, University of Utah School of Medicine

"In her book, *Peaceful Discipline*, Sarah Moore shares a refreshing and easy-to-read-and-implement plan to approach the childrearing years with kindness, improvisation, storytelling, teaching, and a sense of humor. Using storytelling and story teaching to parent is a skill that can be taught, and Moore is an excellent model and creative guide for her readers. Her tone is accessible, warm, nonjudgmental, and even self-deprecating when she generously shares her own mistakes made along the way. I sure wish I had a book like this to help me make better parenting choices when my kids were younger! My household would have been a lot more peaceful!"

—Cynthia C. Muchnick, MA, speaker, educational consultant, and author of *The Everything Guide to Study Skills*, *The Parent Compass: Navigating Your Teen's Wellness and Academic Journey in Today's Competitive World*, and *Writing Successful College Applications*, among others, www.cynthiamuchnick.com

"Sarah has beautifully crafted a book on discipline that is gentle while being clear and kind. It grounds the peaceful parenting approach and will leave you with a feeling of, 'I can do this!'"

—Kim John Payne, MEd, author of *The Soul of Discipline* and *Emotionally Resilient Tweens & Teens*

"Parenting is a journey, and Sarah reminds us that we shape our own stories with our kids through connection; we can change the ending to our stories if we're willing to engage peacefully with ourselves and with our children. Backed by brain-based science, *Peaceful Discipline* provides another powerful tool—story teaching—for every parent's (and teacher's and therapist's) tool belt."

—Dr. Jamie Chaves, OTD, OTR/L, SWC, pediatric occupational therapist

"Parenting offers a firestorm of opportunity for personal awareness and relationship-skills development. This becomes overwhelming when you don't know how to meet an emotion or respond to a challenging behavior. *Peaceful Discipline* offers effortless learning as you turn the pages and grow your understanding of children's needs and behaviors. It actually calmed me down as I read, leaving me more confident, motivated, and resourced with practical things to say or do, so that I can create harmony in the home."

—Andrew Newman, author of *The Hug Who Got Stuck*, www.consciousstories.com

"It really helps to know the *why* behind parenting theories. Sarah covers those in depth, along with concrete and relatable examples of *how* to have more peaceful relationships with our children. This book is practical, fact-based, and filled with real-life tools you can use today. It's shared by a knowledgeable, experienced, and reassuring author. I highly recommend this helpful book."

—Elizabeth Pantley, best-selling author
of *The No-Cry Sleep Solution* series

"A unique contribution to the growing awareness of the benefits of conscious parenting. Sarah Moore's insights can help parents shift from reaction to understanding in reframing their children's behavior. Peaceful is a trait we all need—best cultivated early."

—Raffi Cavoukian, singer, author,
founder of Raffi Foundation for Child Honouring

Peaceful Discipline

Story Teaching, Brain Science & Better Behavior

SARAH R. MOORE

POND READS PRESS

Peaceful Discipline: Story Teaching, Brain Science & Better Behavior

© 2023 by Sarah R. Moore, MFS.
All rights reserved. No part of this book may be reproduced in any form whatsoever, by photography or xerography or by any other means, by broadcast or transmission, by translation into any kind of language, nor by recording electronically or otherwise, without permission in writing from the author, except by a reviewer, who may quote brief passages in critical articles or reviews.

Edited by Kerry Stapley

ISBN 13: 978-1-64343-675-3
Library of Congress Catalog Number: 2022919268
Printed in the United States of America

First Printing: 2023
27 26 25 24 23 5 4 3 2 1

Book design and typesetting by Dan Pitts.
This book is typeset in Didot and CocoSharp font.

Pond Reads Press
939 Seventh Street West
Saint Paul, MN 55102
(952) 829-8818
www.BeaversPondPress.com

To order, visit **dandelion-seeds.com**

Reseller discounts available.

Dedication

To all who strive for peace.

Table of Contents

PREFACE:
HOW ANGER TAUGHT ME TO BE GENTLE

My peaceful parenting journey began about halfway through my daughter's four-month standard medical checkup. She was thriving, ahead on all her milestones. Smiling, rolling, babbling, and snuggling were her favorite pastimes. We were happily growing and learning together; she as a little human, and I as a new mama.

My husband and I had chosen her first pediatrician wisely enough. He was the senior owner of his medical practice and had many years of experience. His wall was covered in accolades and advanced degrees; his résumé included being repeatedly voted as the best pediatrician in our city. A friend of ours used him for all three of her kids and loved him. And, as fate would have it, he happened to be the doctor assigned to check on all the newborns at the hospital the day our daughter was born, so we felt it was a sign that he was right for us.

In his office for that four-month checkup, however, I wasn't so sure. He'd seemed a bit grumpy during our prior visits, but his qualifications being what they were, I'd given him the benefit of the doubt. We're all entitled to bad days; it surely wasn't personal.

We waited for him in the patient room to which we'd been assigned.

He thundered in shortly thereafter and began with, "What questions do you have?"

I offered a "Hi." I asked him something about child development, and he retorted with a quick, "If you'd read the handout the nurse gave you before I came in [he picked it up and shook it for emphasis], you wouldn't be asking things like this."

A bit taken aback, I responded, "Actually, what the nurse handed me is paperwork about two-month milestones, and this is my child's four-month visit. Do you have the paper for her age, please? I'd be happy to read it to see if it answers my question before we continue."

He grabbed the two-month paper and tossed it in the trash, not handing me the alternative, and not answering my question.

Instead, he continued, "How's sleep?"

Responding honestly, I offered, "She had a seven-hour stretch last week for the first time. So, I got a little overconfident. We're up every couple of hours again, but I'm okay with it. She's getting her first tooth a little early and working on lots of new skills. This, too, shall pass. We're happy."

To that, he growled, "You're ridiculous. Don't ever go to her when she cries. She's manipulating you. Let me know when you're ready to get serious about parenting."

Frozen with the unexpected insult, I let him proceed with the rest of her wellness check. Indeed, she was growing and thriving. She was, holistically, getting plenty of sleep. And I was fine with being there for her when she needed me, day or night. I considered it a privilege.

We'd lost her older sister halfway through that pregnancy. *Did he not know how much my heart longed to be there for this child? That going to her when she called was exactly what I wanted to do—that holding and comforting her was the greatest earthly gift I'd ever known?* I was perfectly happy to take sleep day by day.

I spent the next few days feeling livid and replaying the conversation in my mind. I questioned my intuition about picking up my baby, going back and forth in a crazy-making loop. *How dare he imply that I wasn't serious about parenting!* I was fully committed, fully present, and fully engaged in the well-being of my child. She didn't *make* me respond to her; I *chose* to respond because it was my instinct to do so.

I wanted to pick up my baby.

We never saw him again, and we moved on to a much-better-informed and moresensitive pediatrician.

I did not release our interaction emotionally, however. It continued to bother me. I ruminated. My frustration with his inane advice kept growing.

Rather than fight my anger, I decided to lean into it and listen to the message it had to tell. Once I started listening, I realized it was igniting my passion to support other adults in situations similar to mine. It fueled my desire for education about child development. It drove me to encourage new parents to trust themselves, to allow themselves to be physically and emotionally present for their children.

The very next day, I went to the bookstore and bought my first gentle parenting book.

From there, like an Olympic swimmer in training, I dove into all the resources I could find about respectful and positive parenting. I wanted to have all the science, knowledge, and expertise I could possibly find to validate that it is, indeed, a good idea to be kind and responsive to children. (Go figure.)

Our pediatrician planted a seed that day—a desire in me to "get serious about parenting" in a whole new way.

Now, I want to empower other parents to walk out of a situation—be it a doctor's office or anywhere else they don't feel supported—and say, "No. This isn't right. I want better for my child. Where can I find that?"

The Seed Grew—
and Became the Basis for Story Teaching

When I thought about *how* I wanted to support parents, I realized that the best teachers are those who address both the heart and the head. Additionally, I know that we learn best when we feel safe. My desire is that this book will feel right to you intellectually and emotionally, and that it will empower you to teach your children in these same ways.

Sure, some might argue that a scary or upsetting experience taught them an important lesson. However, we learn new things every day. I don't want fear to have a prominent place in my life. I want to feel pretty good most of the time. I'm guessing you and your kids do, too.

Knowing that most people want to feel safe and peaceful every day, *and* knowing that we're learning all the time, we need to find ways to combine our desire for safety with the real-life experience of learning.

How do we learn in safe ways?

- We **observe** the people around us. We learn from others' experiences and figure out which of their experiences we want to try and which seem like bad ideas.
- We **listen** to their guidance, especially if they have expertise in an area that's new to us.
- We **research** the pros and cons of the options we're considering.
- We **try** new things for ourselves, learning what works for us and what doesn't.

Children do these things, too, in their own ways. Naturally, we want to keep them safe and healthy, especially if they're inclined to "leap before they look." We want to help them learn from others' experiences, as well as their own.

A concept I call *story teaching* can help children observe, listen, research, and try new experiences in age-appropriate ways.

Story teaching is, in short, a way to guide and teach our children within the framework of "peaceful discipline." Peaceful discipline is more about us than them; it helps us to be the kinds of parents from whom they can learn without fear. The stories are the teachers; they help us lead, collaborate, and cooperate with one another. They help us express ourselves authentically and say what needs to be said.

Best of all, story teaching is a skill that almost anyone can learn, regardless of age. It helps relationships thrive. I've used stories in every aspect of my life and, most certainly, in my parenting.

Who I Am and How I Know About Storytelling and Parenting

Before you take my word for any of the suggestions you read in this book, I realize you might want to know a thing or two about me.

I received degrees in journalism and French from the University of Wisconsin–Madison (BA, MFS). I then spent nearly twenty years in corporate America, where I'd initially said I'd work for no longer than six months. (Life is funny that way.) I worked extensively in communications, negotiation, conflict resolution, and persuasion—all areas I didn't realize were training me for parenthood!

Partially because I needed a way to offset my stressful workload with some degree of self-care, I also graduated from improvisational comedy school. I attended classes at night after working all day and performed in workshops led by some of the best writers for the late-night American television show *Saturday Night Live*.

Interestingly, professional-level improvisational comedy training directly relates to my knowledge of how to incorporate unpredictability, the importance of play, and "getting into character" with children.

For a variety of reasons, none of which were planned, I ended up leaving my job just a few months after my daughter was born.

Shortly after the birth of my daughter, I also birthed Dandelion Seeds Positive Parenting. At first, it was just a place for me to collect all my research. Eventually, enough people started noticing that I wanted some credentials under my belt.

As a result, I spent a lot of time continuing my professional education—everything from taking interpersonal neurobiology courses with Daniel J. Siegel, MD, and trauma-healing courses with Bessel van der Kolk, MD, to completing certifications with the Jai Institute for Parenting and the Raffi Foundation for Child Honouring.

Having achieved the Master Trainer designation for one of the aforementioned international parenting organizations, I stay up on the latest science of peaceful parenting so that I can accurately and effectively coach parents, grandparents, other caregivers, educators, and medical professionals around the world.

I spent a year in the classroom with world-renowned early childhood expert Teacher Tom, where I watched him interact peacefully with a roomful of excitable preschoolers, navigating group and individual dynamics with ease. I also spent several years working directly with Elizabeth Pantley, a best-selling gentle parenting author and childhood sleep expert.

Now, almost every week, I interview experts in the fields of parenting, neuroscience, attachment, and child development so that I can explore a wide range of different perspectives firsthand. In other words, I choose to surround myself with good, smart, wise humans who deeply understand children.

I also spend a lot of time writing for international parenting magazines. Now, with hundreds of thousands of readers around the world (a fact that still blows my mind), I'm committed to delivering research-based and accurate information. I want my readers to trust that my guidance is based on science and is not just the opinion of some random mama on the Internet. Along with this, I've been chosen as a partner in the Trusted Parenting Network for the American Society for the Positive Care of Children (American SPCC).

Above all, I want to be clear on one thing: I am not here for the social media followers or any fleeting recognition. Peaceful parenting is the message I want to promote, regardless of whose account you check every morning (although I do very much appreciate your support).

My greatest motivation, of course, has always been my own child. She's the bright light that deeply and sincerely motivates me to get parenting as "right" as I possibly can. If I don't do that in my own life, what would be the point?

I'm here for you. At the most fundamental level, my heartfelt desire is to make the world more loving. I sincerely believe that positive, respectful, trust-based, and collaborative parenting is where it all needs to start. Will you join me?

What You'll Learn in this Book

You didn't come here for the snacks, right? In this book, you'll not only learn how stories make excellent nonpunitive teachers for our kids but *why* they do. Just as young children are prone to ask, "Why?" adults want to see it to believe it. I'll show you the why.

I'll share the science behind my recommendations, and you'll learn lots of ways to have a more positive and connected relationship with your children. You'll discover ways to stay calm even when you're angry or frustrated. You'll also hear about ways to increase connection and cooperation with your kids without yelling at them or shaming them. You might just go to sleep at night feeling downright good about your parenting.

You'll learn some of what's going on in your brain as well as in your children's brains so that you can connect more naturally, and as a result, more joyfully. Joy really can be our natural state of living together.

Furthermore, I share lots of personal examples of times these ideas have worked in my own family (as well as the times I've completely missed the mark)!

This book will culminate in a series of stories that you can use with your children. These stories will not only help you parent peacefully and tell your own stories but will also help your kids exhibit the kinds of behavior you want to see.

At the end, you'll find resources that have helped me on my own parenting journey. I know many of these authors personally and can say without hesitation they're really good and decent humans.

In the meantime, I thank you for being one of the good and decent humans striving to be gentle with your children. That's why we're all here. This work matters.

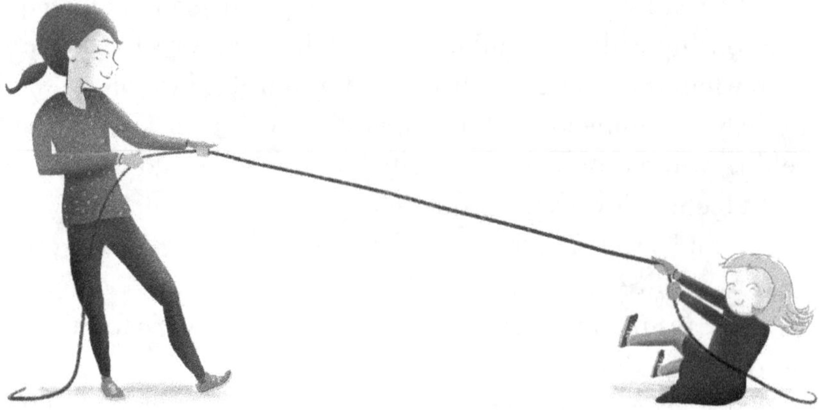

Part 1:

THE BASIS FOR STORYTELLING AND STORY TEACHING

CHAPTER 1:

WHY WE NEED TOOLS THAT WORK—AND DON'T MAKE US FEEL LIKE JERKS

I've heard from countless parents that they're struggling. Here's an example of a scenario that plays out in various forms in homes all over the world.

A parent walks into their child's bedroom and finds the child, for no clear reason, pulling all the clothing out of the drawers and throwing the items haphazardly across the floor.

Without missing a beat, the parent yells, "What are you doing? Stop it! Put these clothes away right this second! Sheesh—I just folded them! What are you trying to do to me?" The parent then storms out, warning the child they have five minutes to make the room spotless or there will be negative consequences.

The frustration is certainly justified. Who wants to put away laundry once, let alone twice?

At the same time, the child likely feels small after having been yelled at by their trusted big person. The child may or may not know why they were throwing the laundry. (Boredom? Curiosity? Temporary loss of marbles, literally or figuratively?) The child may also feel afraid—perhaps of the punishment itself, or perhaps of their perceived loss of connection with their parent. Either way, the child feels distant, helpless, and small—and likely sad or resentful.

Soon thereafter, the parent may have collected him- or herself and now feels like a jerk, having yelled for what feels like the hundredth time that week. They hate the way their outbursts seem to drive a wedge between them and their child, *even when their feelings are justified*. The guilt feels heavy and oppressive. They want a better path forward, but where to start? Is change even possible, much less change to which the child will actually respond?

Although the details might differ, we've all been there. Just when everything is moving along peacefully, our child throws us for a loop. They do something we wish they hadn't. We flip out. It's mayhem. Very, very uncomfortable mayhem, and it feels like a lost cause. All we wanted was to sit back for a second and take a breath, and now *this* happens (whatever *this* is).

Why can't things just be easier? Can we actually like our child and feel sure that they like us back?

I hear you, and I get it. And I'm here with hope and encouragement for you—along with some very practical tools that will help you catch that breath (and exhale it fully, deeply, and calmly).

Parenting doesn't have to be as hard as it sometimes seems. We can find peace. More than that, we can create peace—through a wonderful tool I call *story teaching*. Story teaching is exactly what it sounds like: teaching our children through both real and made-up stories. I'll explain more about it in the next chapter.

To be clear, story teaching is one of many peaceful parenting tools. By itself, it's not enough for every situation. However, when we couple story teaching with a deeper understanding of brain science and child development, we can transform chaos and pain into something substantially lighter for us and for our children.

This book will show you how. It's a guide for creating a more joyful (and less stressful) life with your kids. It's filled with actionable and specific tools that can improve your relationships, and with the *why* behind what we're doing.

In the *why* lies the key to creating lasting change in our hearts.

Later in this book, I'll revisit the scenario above without judgment, but with better ideas for how to handle it.

I'll also get into why our approach matters so much, not only for us as parents but also for our kids' optimal development.

This is a story for you, dear parents, to make your life easier. To help you parent without guilt, shame, or hurt feelings. To help you give and receive love in all the most peaceful and nurturing ways, because you and your children deserve to live that way.

CHAPTER 2:

UNDERSTANDING STORYTELLING AND STORY TEACHING

If you were here for a history lesson, I'd tell you that storytelling for the purpose of teaching has been used throughout human existence. Inuit and Mayan cultures used storytelling to guide their children and teach them about everything from water safety to how to manage emotions. Other storytelling cultures included Choctaw, Hawaiian, Jewish, West African, and Irish, among others. You'll find references to storytelling in the Bible, where Jesus used parables to teach his disciples. The list of storytellers throughout history is extensive, but there's a consistent thread: all used the power of story as a benign and gentle tool to help others learn in a way that is peaceful and effective.

I'm guessing you're not here for the history lesson, though. You're probably here because you're seeking ways to support your kids and make parenting a bit easier. If so, good news! Without a doubt, storytelling can help you do these things.

If it works and causes no harm, though, why isn't storytelling more common?

Frankly, modern parents have generally opted for quick fixes and convenience. To be fair, some of these do serve a valid purpose in parenting. We've got plenty to do as it is, right? At the same time, there are some very compelling reasons to bring back storytelling as a teaching tool.

If you're thinking this is going to take a long time and require a lot of effort—hold on! Although there's literally enough information to write a book about teaching through stories, I will also be sharing other companion tools that will help you on your parenting journey.

Working with the whole package of tools, including teaching through stories, is life-changing. When you invest some time integrating these tools into your parenting, you'll ultimately save huge amounts of time and energy. You'll have far fewer battles in your life.

Plus, the storytelling process itself is really quite straightforward. Best of all, it works.

Why does storytelling work?

At the risk of stating the obvious, we know this for sure: **kids like stories**! That's part of the reason people have been telling them for more than thirty thousand years.

Science-wise, we know from brilliant parenting books like *The Power of Showing Up* by Daniel J. Siegel, MD, and Tina Payne Bryson, PhD, that kids thrive most when they feel the four S's: safe, seen, soothed, and secure. Storytime on a parent's lap is often a place where all four of those S's grow and coexist quite naturally. It's no wonder kids like it so much.

Perhaps a bit less obvious: stories help children understand and better navigate their feelings, while also helping develop their executive function skills (more about those soon). Storytelling, as separate from real-life experience, is a way for children to learn in emotionally safe ways with little to no emotional risk.

Although nearly all kids like stories, they're particularly well-suited to sensitive kids who could get emotionally flooded by other forms of correction.

Beyond the fact that kids like stories—and beyond some basic science of why they do—there's still more to consider. For instance, children's creativity is declining in alarming, measurable ways—especially between kindergarten and third grade—yet storytelling demonstrates dynamic ways to use our imaginations. Through storytelling, we engage our kids in ways that strengthen and nurture their creativity. The imagination should never become a lost art.

After all, we're not just entertaining them with stories (although we should certainly do some of that); we're teaching them in a form that elicits their innate curiosity. We're transitioning from passive entertainment to active participation. In their own way, stories help reawaken a sacred part of childhood.

In addition to nurturing their creativity, interactive storytelling with an adult can offer children **protective measures** against some potentially troubling outcomes.

Just for the sake of argument, let's talk about excess screen time for a moment. (Again, no judgment. My child sometimes watches her shows while I write.)

Two quick but important points to consider:

1. We're all human. For many families, screens serve a very real and valuable purpose. I'm not suggesting we do away with them. They're clearly here to stay! What matters is that we use them responsibly and not as a replacement for human interaction. Plus, there are some beneficial online activities and programs, such as the cartoon *Daniel Tiger's Neighborhood*. This cartoon, intended for preschool-aged children, addresses many topics related to social-emotional intelligence. It's one on a very short list of shows that's been studied and linked to specific positive outcomes for children:

    > Children . . . who watched *Daniel Tiger's Neighborhood* had higher levels of empathy, were generally better at recognizing emotions, and were more confident in social situations than the children who only watched [a] nature television show [in the study].[1]

1 "Study Shows Daniel Tiger's Neighborhood Helps Kids Learn Important Life Lessons," Children's International Pediatrics, November 22, 2019, https://cimgpeds.com/study-shows-daniel-tigers-neighborhood-helps-kids-learn-important-life-lessons/.

Can a cartoon really do all that? Sort of, but not entirely. These positive results don't happen through osmosis. We need to talk to our kids about what they're watching for the benefits to kick in.

> Children experienced the above benefits only when their parents regularly talked with them about what's on television or YouTube. In other words, the researchers found that it was the combination of watching *Daniel Tiger's Neighborhood* and the conversations parents had with the kids about the show that produced increases in social skills. It was clear that neither letting the child watch the show alone, nor a conversation alone, was enough. It takes both watching and discussion to have positive results.[2]

Although nature shows may contribute to "book knowledge" (information to memorize), *Daniel Tiger* empowers children with life skills they can use to get along with others—not only in the preschool years but also as the foundation for many social interactions they'll have on an ongoing basis. It's a different kind of learning that people often call "emotional intelligence."

2. Few adults will feel comfortable (or able) to tell stories for hours per week (the equivalent of "lost" screen time). I wrote this book, and I'm certainly not making up two hours of stories per day! The point is that active engagement of some sort serves a very good purpose, and part of that time can be storytelling.

2 Erica Rasmussen, "How Daniel Tiger Helps Teach Social Skills to Preschoolers," PBS, July 8, 2016, https://www.pbs.org/parents/thrive/how-daniel-tiger-helps-teach-social-skills-to-preschoolers.

Sneak preview of later sections of this book: stories come in lots of forms. Many of those forms are much easier for parents than we think. More on that soon; we may get to our two hours per day without even realizing it. These two hours do not need to be consecutive or difficult. Ten-minute increments count! Plus, we can still keep some screen time if we want to.

You may be surprised to learn that quality time spent interacting with children can offer protective measures for parents, too.

First, though, some stats about why we—the parents—need something to change:

Although 91 percent of adults [with children] say parenting is their greatest joy, 73 percent also say that raising children is their biggest challenge. Of those 73 percent, 69 percent say they'd use more positive parenting strategies if they had them, but right now, they simply don't have them.[3] Moreover, "75 percent of parents with kids under age eighteen . . . said their stress [has] increased since the COVID-19 pandemic."

In short, things aren't getting easier for parents. They're struggling—unnecessarily.

Need more?

Parents are just plain burned out from parenting, and the numbers aren't going in the right direction. In the United States, for example, roughly 80 percent of parents currently report burnout.[4] That's eighty out of one hundred moms and dads who just feel . . . done. Depleted. Ready to check out. This is a problem beyond everyday annoyance.

Is the antidote to parental burnout time away from the kids, then?

---

3 "Zero to Three National Parent Survey and Key Insights," CI Learn, June 2016, https://cilearn.csuci.edu/courses/27/pages/zero-to-three-national-parent-survey-overview-and-key-insights.

4 Peter Dockrill, "Parental Burnout in the US is Among the Highest in the World, And We May Know Why," Science Alert, September 24, 2021, https://www.sciencealert.com/parental-burnout-in-the-us-is-among-the-highest-in-the-world.

Sure, we all need a break sometimes. However, what we may need more is to improve the *quality* of our time with our children, especially since most of us don't have the luxury of a break anytime we want one. We must consciously and actively engage in activities that increase joy within each other's presence.

In fact, spending uninterrupted quality time may be the key to avoiding a whole host of problems, thereby making our lives easier, not harder. As for the protective measures I mentioned, here's what we know. According to Jones (2017),

> Children [who spend quality time with their parents] are less likely to have behavioral issues at home or at school. Children who are spending more quality time with their families are less likely to participate in risky behaviors, such as drug and alcohol usage. Showing your children that you love and care for them helps to keep them mentally and emotionally strong. For parents, the best way to do this is to spend quality time with them on a regular basis. Children who spend more quality time with their families are more likely to be physically healthy (Rider, 2018). Overall, spending quality time with your children is important to them, but is also important to your own well-being. [5]

If we can escape having to deal with some avoidable behavioral challenges, risky behaviors, and health issues, our lives automatically become easier. That, in turn, can reduce burnout and chronic stress. Sign me up!

Back to stories, though—they're very much a part of this quality time.

Perhaps most importantly, guiding children with our presence, spending meaningful time together, and using peaceful discipline strategies help us connect with and guide them in ways that **do no harm.**

---

5 Claire Roudabush, "Why Spending Quality Time with Your Children Is Important," South Dakota State, last modified April 9, 2019, https://extension.sdstate.edu/why-spending-quality-time-your-children-important.

Stories, by definition, are naturally connecting and nonpunitive. A nonpunitive approach is truly the heart of positive parenting; **it's parenting with the good of the relationship in mind.**

The Difference Between Storytelling and Story Teaching

Throughout this book, I will refer to storytelling as *story teaching*. My aim is to differentiate between storytelling for the pure enjoyment of it, which in and of itself holds tremendous value, and story teaching, the goal of which is to help grow our children's emotional intelligence. Nurturing their emotional intelligence helps kids learn how to get along well in the world. After all, we're doing our best to raise decent, loving humans. That's the end goal.

We'll look at story teaching from three angles:

- **Preventative:** These stories help children prepare for situations that might otherwise be tricky for them. (Examples: a child who has social anxiety going to a birthday party, or a child whose "normal" exuberant behavior might not be perceived well at, say, a family wedding.)

Why this matters:

According to Harvard University's Center on the Developing Child, children's brains are growing at approximately one million new neural connections per second.[6] (Wow!) The more we can prepare these brains for what to expect by talking about situations beforehand, the more we can facilitate that incredible brain growth. These connections are reinforced through both the child's understanding of the experiences and the experiences themselves.

---

6 "Brain Architecture," Center on the Developing Child, Harvard University, August 20, 2019, https://developingchild.harvard.edu/science/key-concepts/brain-architecture/.

- **In the Moment:** These stories help ground children when they're struggling and help increase their social-emotional skills. (Examples: a child who teases another child on the playground and whose caregiver wants to intercept the behavior without shaming or embarrassing the child; a child who's struggling with school drop-off.)

Why this matters:

According to the Together for Kids Coalition, "Emotional well-being and social competence provide a strong foundation for emerging cognitive abilities, and together they are the bricks and mortar of brain architecture. The emotional and physical health, social skills, and cognitive-linguistic capacities that emerge in the early years are all important for success in school, the workplace, and in the larger community." [7]

- **Restorative:** These are stories that children use to make sense of events that have already transpired but that might cause ongoing toxic stress or trauma if left unresolved. (Examples: a child who unexpectedly lost a pet, a relative, or a home, or who has ongoing peer-related struggles at school.)

Why this matters:

"Healthy" amounts of stress can be motivating. (For example, if we want to run well in the race, we push ourselves to train for it.) This kind of stress is not only normal but beneficial. It helps our kids learn that they can do hard things, are resilient, and have grit. Dr. Mona Delahooke tells us in *Brain-Body Parenting* that "children learn and grow best from their hardships through their parents' loving support," and Drs. Michele Borba (in *Thrivers*) and Sam Goldstein and Robert B. Brooks (in *Tenacity in Children*) devote entire books to helping kids thrive despite adversity.

---

7 Together for Kids Coalition, "Pillars of a Healthy Childhood," Together for Kids Coalition (2022).

However, *toxic* stress is problematic. Toxic stress is ongoing stress without resolution. Harvard's Center on the Developing Child defines toxic stress as strong, frequent, or prolonged adversity, which is damaging to children's development.[8] Here's what can happen if it's left unresolved:

> Toxic stress weakens the architecture of the developing brain, which can lead to lifelong problems in learning, behavior, and physical and mental health. Experiencing stress is an important part of healthy development. Activation of the stress response produces a wide range of physiological reactions that prepare the body to deal with threat. However, when these responses remain activated at high levels for significant periods of time without supportive relationships to help calm them, toxic stress results. This can impair the development of neural connections, especially in the areas of the brain dedicated to higher-order skills.

Restorative stories can help mitigate daily stressors so that children don't get overwhelmed with excessive emotional burdens. They can process their struggles in healthy ways and then move on from them, without allowing stress to linger and, possibly, become toxic.

I'll cover **preventative, in-the-moment**, and **restorative** story teaching, as well as what to do with the sometimes emotionally messy space beneath a child's suboptimal behavior, their big feelings; and their ability to make better choices in the future.

Finally, just so you know: I'll refer to "parents" and "parenting" in these pages, but that's simply my shorthand for referring to *all* the wonderful and loving caregivers—family and otherwise—who help raise children. I see and appreciate all of you.

---

8 "Toxic Stress," Center for the Developing Child, Harvard University, August 17, 2022, https://developingchild.harvard.edu/science/key-concepts/toxic-stress/.

Oh, and a bonus PS here: the various phenomena, behaviors, thoughts, emotions, and processes described in this book may not apply to all neurodiverse or neurotypical children, or children with other unique physical, mental, or emotional differences. You know your child best, and I encourage all caregivers to seek professional support if they need it.

One More Quick Note Before We Dive In: Imperfect Parenting Is Normal, Healthy Parenting

Guaranteed, we will trip up along the way. I know I have. In fact, when I told my daughter I was writing a parenting book, she innocently and sincerely asked, "Is it about how to make mistakes?" Apparently, I've nailed *that* bit of this mama gig!

It's important for you to know how perfectly normal it is to be imperfect. If you make mistakes like I do, you're my people. I want you to firmly know this before you read through the "should" and "how to" examples in this book. Just do the best you can.

That's what I'm doing over here. My child will attest to that.

Even more than that, I *want* you to mess up sometimes. When we mess up, we model for our kids what it means to be human and how to recover from our mistakes. That's a life skill they'll need to master *with your help.* (Who'd want to grow up in a home with "perfect" adults, anyway?) You're their safe place where they can practice being human and learn to repair their mistakes. Mistakes aren't shortcomings. They're teachers.

CHAPTER 3:

EMOTION COACHING AND EXECUTIVE FUNCTION SKILLS

If you're already well versed in emotion coaching, proactively helping your children to "keep their calm," and nurturing your child's executive function skills, you're welcome to hop on over to part 3. You can return to this part of the book as a reference when necessary.

This section describes the *why* of many of the elements that story teaching encompasses—as well as the *how* of some specific scenarios that promote brain development in children.

I'll show you how to navigate a triggering event (if there is one), the child's big feelings, and how to seize learning opportunities.

Understanding these topics can help you create stories that are more likely to achieve your objectives.

If this is new information to you, or if you'd like another take on what you already know, this section can offer you a new or different perspective.

What Is Emotion Coaching?

Emotion coaching enables children to understand what they're feeling and why. It gives them tools to navigate their emotions and process them in healthy ways. It normalizes and creates a safe place for full expression of whatever they're experiencing. From there, they can learn better emotional regulation skills.

Although emotional regulation skills are multifaceted and complex, the short description is that they reflect a person's ability to refrain from acting out in the moment.

Emotional regulation skills grow in the pause that happens between thought and action, wherein we process how we're *instinctively driven* to react versus how we *want* to respond.

Better emotional regulation means fewer instances of outbursts and other tricky behavior. To be able to regulate emotions, of course, children have to know what emotions *are* in the first place.

Despite the myriad synonyms for them, and various combinations and nuances thereof, there are only six main categories of emotions:[9]

- Happiness
- Sadness
- Fear
- Disgust
- Anger
- Surprise

Why Does Emotion Coaching Matter?

With emotion coaching, we give our children something to *do* with their feelings. It's a road map for managing their emotions in healthy ways. We're showing how to navigate feelings, to embrace them, to befriend and welcome them as part of living a peaceful life among other humans.

Managing emotions healthily is a skill that will benefit all the child's relationships throughout their life.

A regulated child can always learn better and more easily than a dysregulated one.

---

9 Kendra Cherry, "The 6 Types of Basic Emotions and their Effect on Human Behavior," Verywell Mind, last modified April 05, 2021, https://www.verywellmind.com/an-overview-of-the-types-of-emotions-4163976.

How Does Emotion Coaching Work?

When a child is very young, a parent can help the child learn about their feelings in three key ways:

- By modeling and describing their own emotions. Example: "I'm crying because I feel sad."
- By labeling and discussing the child's emotions. Example: "You feel happy. I can tell by the big smile on your face."
- By labeling and discussing others' emotions. Example: "This character in your book feels mad. I can tell because his face is red and he's scowling."

As the child grows older and/or more emotionally mature, you can add detail and complexity to the discussion:

- "I'm crying because I feel **sad**. I'm lonely for Grandma. I miss her."
- "You feel **happy** that we're playing together. I can tell by the big smile on your face. I'm curious if you're also feeling excited and relieved because we can play all day without having to go anywhere."
- "The character in your book feels **mad**. I can tell because his face is red and he's scowling. I wonder if he also feels embarrassed because everyone is looking at him and pointing."

I refrain from including specific ages to represent a "young" child versus an "older" one, because each child differs in their emotional literacy and in their comfort in talking about emotions. Heck, plenty of adults are uncomfortable talking about feelings!

Some kids, of course, don't like having adults label their feelings for them, especially feelings like anger and sadness. Why is this?

For one thing, our timing is sometimes off. Have you ever been in the midst of feeling something BIG and someone else, albeit with good intentions, kept trying to interrupt with their analysis of your situation? Likewise, children want the space to *feel* what they're feeling without it being a topic of discussion right then and there (which involves using a very different part of the brain). The feeling is still too raw for them. Although every experience can be a teachable moment, not everything *should* be a teachable moment. Sometimes the experience itself is enough . . . for now.

Another common source of pushback is when the child doubts that their adult "gets" their reason for being upset. If this is the case, they may feel extra vulnerable, and the added vulnerability of having their adult talk about it on top of their already big feelings can be too much to process. They may feel like, "My special big person doesn't understand my point of view, and they'll probably just tell me I'm wrong for feeling this way, so why bother?"

In both cases, a parent's best bet may be to wait until the child calms down a bit before analyzing or naming anything. Show them you're on their side by listening without judging. Trust that what they feel is true for them, even if it makes no sense to you. Keep an open mind while your child speaks without rushing to teach them anything, and they'll be much more likely to open up to you.

Debriefing in a nonjudgmental way *after* the emotional storm has passed can create the safety children need to let others help them identify and label their feelings. Once you do this, your child is likely to be much more receptive to talking about their emotions.

If you happen to be that adult who struggles to talk about feelings, or perhaps even to feel them at all, start small. Name and acknowledge when you feel everyday bodily sensations, such as "I'm hot" or "I'm thirsty" or "I have to use the restroom." The more you can become sensitive to your body on the most basic levels, the more you make feeling anything at all a bit safer. This approach can help kids who don't love talking about their feelings, as well.

If emotions really don't feel safe to you, you can do wonderfully productive work with a parent coach or therapist that can help you develop greater inner safety. For kids, play therapy can help.

If a child is unpredictable in their willingness to talk about feelings, know that is normal! Child development is not linear. What might work emotionally for a child one day might not work at all for that same child the very next day (or even later that same day). Just as emotions are fluid and dynamic, so is the child's ability to acknowledge, comprehend, and work through them.

You'll see this unpredictability in their behavior as well. Lots of factors play into the child's ability to repeatedly act in a consistent manner. For example, the child's emotional state, physical sensations (tiredness, hunger, thirst), sensory needs, and other influences vary day by day. These variations in children (and adults) are normal.

Not to mention, children's brains are still growing at incredible rates and forming new neural connections all the time. It takes years for the child's brain to master what they "should" be doing. (Show me the adult whose behavior is 100 percent consistent and predictable, while we're at it.)

How Else Can We Support Our Children's Emotional Development?

We can allow—and better, create—many opportunities for joy.

The more joy and emotional peace are our "defaults" with our kids, the more they'll become our children's defaults, too.

If, for example, we choose to take life (and ourselves) a little less seriously, our kids will mimic that as they grow older. They'll learn not to sweat the small stuff, and rather, they'll seek out experiences that contribute to their overall sense of well-being. Even better, when that's their default, they'll pass that gift along to others. Happiness is contagious in beautiful ways.

We can infuse play into the mundane. We can laugh and dance and sing together. We can model a glass-half-full attitude, even when life is imperfect and messy.

An example:

One night, I was exceptionally tired and didn't feel like cooking, but I somehow mustered up the barely-there energy to throw a decent meal into the oven. Once it was cooked, I went to retrieve it, looking forward to little more than going to sleep.

As I pulled it out of the oven, however, I dropped it, and it landed upside down on the floor. It was a colossal hot mess, and I was tempted to follow suit. My daughter rushed over and was clearly waiting to see how I'd respond.

Keeping myself in check, I spoke to the floor: "Oh, floor! If you were hungry, you could've just asked me for dinner! You didn't need to go and steal my food. Oh dear."

My child cracked up. There was nothing I could do about my mistake—I don't think a three-second rule applies to a 350-degree pile of food that's splattered across the hardwoods. So, we dealt with it.

Not only did we not keel over from having cereal for dinner that one night (far from it), but my child also likely learned that we get to choose how we want to respond to unfortunate situations. This was a prime opportunity to model the "no big deal" attitude I want her to embrace and keep for when she inevitably ruins something of her own someday.

Do I always handle it so gracefully? Heck no! Sometimes I crumble and grumble, just like everybody else. And that's okay, too. What matters most is that my child will have more than one option of how to react in her mind when she's there herself.

We can allow and encourage cathartic tears when the child is sad, which creates nonjudgmental space for their feelings. We can refrain from offering quick solutions or distractions.

- We can replace "Don't cry" with "I'm here for you. Let it out."

- We can do the work to release our own discomfort around our child's tears, knowing that by allowing those tears to flow freely, the child is washing away their hurts.

- We can honor the child's experience. While we might be tempted to find humor in a child's sadness that their favorite blade of grass was mown down, we can trust that their feelings are as real to them as ours are to us. (I once held a funeral for my child's beloved roly-poly [potato bug] that she'd discovered in our garden. She mourned and woke up crying for two nights after its passing. It was a very real loss for her.)

We can model healthy anger management strategies, including journaling, exercising, and using "*I*" statements rather than blaming or shaming "*you*" statements during conflict. We can practice pausing before reacting to situations that anger us. We can verbalize to our children why we're doing these things.

- We can replace "You did WHAT? You're making me crazy!" with "I'm feeling frustrated. I'm going to take some deep breaths until I feel more peaceful again."

- We can stop thinking of the child as having disobeyed when they've done something we don't like. If we think in terms of disobedience, our tendency is to want the opposite—to make them "obey." If we reword and reframe "disobeyed" to the child feeling "dysregulated," we can remember that the opposite is "regulated"—and that the solution is to help them find their calm. I'll share more about this in a second.

We can encourage our children to seek support when they need it, understanding that co-regulation,[10] rather than self-regulation, is what ultimately supports the child's ability to cope well during stress or difficulty.

What is co-regulation?

Co-regulation is when we stay present physically and emotionally alongside our child to help them process their feelings, rather than send them away for so-called self-soothing.

The way children learn to self-soothe is by practicing calming strategies alongside their trusted adults.[11] There's no age by which children must be able to consistently accomplish this on their own.

Even adults often seek out other adults for support when they're feeling particularly upset or bothered by something. Because children learn through repeated practice with an adult, in time, they'll begin to emulate what they've learned from us. They'll begin to find their own peace without always needing us for support.

Again, of course, like all things in child development, this process isn't linear—it's developmentally healthy and normal to need connection and support from others throughout our lives. No one thrives in an emotional vacuum.

We can also teach our child ways to calm and regulate their body throughout the day—called proprioceptive tools[12]—and these are especially effective when a child already has healthy emotional regulation.

---

10 K. D. Rosanbalm and D. W. Murray, "Caregiver Co-regulation Across Development: A Practice Brief," US Department of Health and Human Services (October 2017).

11 Blair Paley and Nastassia J. Hajal, "Conceptualizing Emotion Regulation as Family-Level Phenomena," Pub Med Central, National Library of Medicine, January 30, 2022, https://www.ncbi.nlm.nih.gov/pmc/articles/PMC8801237/.

12 Tal Shafir, "Using Movement to Regulate Emotion: Neurophysiological Findings and their Application in Psychotherapy," Frontiers in Psychology, Frontiers, September 23, 2016, https://www.frontiersin.org/articles/10.3389/fpsyg.2016.01451/full.

What Are Proprioceptive Tools?

Proprioceptive tools are ways the child can check in with their body throughout the day to help encourage emotional regulation. They work by keeping the child in touch with their own body, both in times of stress and times of calm. Neurologically, this process engages the parasympathetic nervous system (the part that calms us down) to help children reduce anxiety[13] and remain calm.

Examples of proprioceptive tools include the following:

- Small muscle movements, like giving oneself a hand or arm massage or hugging oneself around the midsection. Deep belly breathing is also a helpful proprioceptive tool to use throughout the day. These are beneficial for ongoing feelings of calm when the child is feeling regulated—and that help them stay that way.

- Large muscle movements, like pushing hard against an immobile object (a countertop, a wall, pushing downward on a chair while seated). Deep stretching is also beneficial when the child is feeling unsettled.

Additionally, breathwork can be incredibly calming for the nervous system. The tricky part is, however, that if you advise a screaming child to "take a deep breath," you might as well tell the sun not to shine. Kids in a state of heightened dysregulation aren't capable of going into their "rational" brain and thinking, *Oh, dear me, my-wonderful-and-ever-patient-saint of a parent, my feelings simply got carried away. I'll get on top of those nice, calming breaths straightaway!*

So, how do you get children to use the incredible power of their breath if they're not having it? Try speaking in kid terms. Instead of "belly breaths," invite them to

13 Chelsea Long, "How the Parasympathetic Nervous System Can Lower Stress," Hospital for Special Surgery, August 30, 2021, https://www.hss.edu/article_parasympathetic-nervous-system.asp.

- Pretend they're blowing the biggest bubble they've ever blown through a bubble wand
- Be a fire-breathing dragon (this works especially well when the child is angry!)
- Pretend they're an alligator swimming in a lagoon and they need to use the breath in their whole body to propel themselves forward through the water
- Envision they're a rocket ship about to blast off and they need to push their breath out from the bottoms of their feet to propel themselves into outer space
- Buzz like a bee
- Hum like a hummingbird or make race car sounds
- Sing the longest, loudest note they can (perhaps time it and see if they can beat their personal best)

An Example:

At my daughter's dental appointment a few months ago, she decided about twenty seconds into her cleaning that she was unequivocally done. Hmmmm. Houston, we have a problem.

Fortunately, the hygienist was patient and supportive, yet she understandably wanted to move on to her next patient and keep everyone on schedule.

After logic and reason proved to be fruitless with my child (whose lower lip was now starting to tremble), I remembered belly breaths. I asked her if she thought she could blow me out the window.

Huh?

"Yes," I said, "please blow me out the window. I'd love to go for a quick fly around the block." My daughter, being curious, blew the biggest breath she could possibly exhale in my direction. I pretended to flail backward toward the window, but quickly regained my balance. She thought it was funny, so she tried again, harder this time.

Before she knew it, she'd taken five great belly breaths under the guise of blowing me out the window. Giggling and without further prompting, she told the hygienist she could continue.

All these child-friendly relaxation techniques engage the vagus nerve, thereby promoting near-immediate relaxation.[14] Most children, of course, couldn't care less about a vagus whatever-it-is. What they'll know is that, suddenly, they feel better. It's like magic! Important note: the magic isn't always immediate or, well, magical—but any step closer to calm can feel like a win for the parent and the child.

One more breathing tip: as naturally as breathing happens when kids (and adults) are regulated, we all tend to hold our breath / hyperventilate / breathe anything but naturally when we're upset. Practice these breathing techniques when the child is calm and fully regulated. That way, they won't give you the side eye when you bring up "dragon breaths" while they're upset. It'll be familiar terminology for them.

More importantly, it'll be a familiar body practice for them. They'll have muscle memory, and it will come more naturally this way.

Why not just have them count to ten when they're mad or stressed like many of us have been taught to do?

If that works for you or your child, great! For most kids, though, when they're having a body response (yelling, acting out, feeling big things), they need a body solution. It takes some pretty strong presence of mind to remember to count to ten, much less gain the benefits by being in the right mindset for it. Even then, it may not work. I know it's still not my go-to when I'm on the verge of flipping out.

Personally, when I try to count to ten, I often end up thinking, *Great. Now I'm still mad, and I just wasted time counting to ten.*

---

14 "5 Ways to Stimulate Your Vagus Nerve," Health Essentials, Cleveland Clinic, March 10, 2022, https://health.clevelandclinic.org/vagus-nerve-stimulation/.

No bueno. My body needs to feel safe and peaceful from the inside out.

Here's why we often need body solutions, scientifically: when we're emotionally triggered, the limbic system (a more primitive part of the brain) takes over and effectively shuts off the frontal lobe, where most of our rational thoughts live. The limbic system's sole purpose is to keep us alive. The frontal lobe is where we can think about others' experiences, offer compassion, and understand the consequences of our actions. The limbic system doesn't understand that we'll ever be all right again, because it's not planning ahead—it's trying to keep us safe in this moment only. Our goal, therefore, is to help the body feel safety so that our frontal lobe can come back and join the whole brain party. No one can talk us into safety if our limbic system is overriding it; we must feel it for ourselves.

No matter which calming tools they use, these approaches can help make the child more receptive to learning through story teaching and other forms of positive discipline that strengthen their executive function skills.

What Are Executive Function Skills?

This section addresses the *why* of story teaching. Just like we want to know why we should ride a bike before randomly getting on a two-wheeled piece of metal, executive function is *why* we story teach in the first place.

Executive function refers to a set of skills that children develop over time through the natural course of their development to manage things like impulse control, emotional expression, patience, and the ability to think about the consequences of their actions. Understandably, these are skills that parents very much want their children to develop.

Executive function skills grow in the frontal lobes of the brain, most notably the prefrontal cortex. Perhaps to parents' chagrin, the prefrontal cortex is not fully developed until approximately age twenty-five.[15] Until that magical age, kids are prone to lacking patience, having big emotional releases, and having difficulty managing their impulses. Although we can help them practice these skills, there's not much they can do about these challenges until they get older. There's simply no rushing time and development, just like we can't make a flower bloom faster by watering it more.

To be sure, the child's underdeveloped brain can be a source of stress for people who believe the child should be able to perform certain tasks repeatedly and consistently before their brain is physically able to allow that to happen.

We might, for example, have a child who's well rested, well nourished, and emotionally regulated and, therefore, agreeable and cooperative when asked to go brush their teeth. In Dr. Mona Delahooke's book *Brain-Body Parenting*, she refers to a child like this as being on the "green pathway." Because of their position of feeling emotionally secure in the moment, this child might be able to carry out the requested task without parental support. The child thinks, *Sure! I'll go brush my teeth! I've got this!*

However, the very next night, if that same child is overtired or overstimulated, the child might not feel *emotionally* able to brush their teeth. Sure, they're physically capable of holding a toothbrush, but they might be emotionally unable to proceed without their special adult nearby.

Indeed, something as simple to adults as toothbrushing can feel legitimately stressful to a child. This is not about a child being willful or stubborn. The child's struggle is as real as any of our adult-size struggles might be. If the child refuses, it's often not because they *won't*; it may be a legitimate *can't*. They may have entered what Dr. Delahooke calls the "red pathway," where they may fight back and be combative. Or maybe they enter the "blue pathway," where they simply shut down. Either way, the

15 Mariam Arain et al., "Maturation of the Adolescent Brain," Dove Medical Press, April 3, 2013, https://www.dovepress.com/maturation-of-the-adolescent-brain-peer-reviewed-fulltext-article-NDT.

limbic system is effectively overriding all the capabilities they could manage without incident the night before. They're doing their best with the resources they have at the time.

The same is true for the other parts of developing executive function skills. For example, a child who's normally quite patient might have an errant day where they simply can't sit still and wait. Their brain isn't letting them focus. The next day, they might have no trouble with patience or delayed gratification.

Understanding and accepting the unpredictability of brain development and emerging executive function skills can help adults establish more realistic expectations. However, on days we know our kids are low on sleep or whatever they need, we *can* predict that they are likely to struggle more with the basic things we ask of them.

Along with this, young children who are dysregulated are often told to "use their words" when they're upset. As you've likely noticed, it doesn't always work. Perhaps the child was able to articulate their stress yesterday, but they can't today—they're just falling apart emotionally. Their executive function skills are struggling.

When it comes to using their words, the part of their brain that controls language (the Broca's area) has been sent "offline" by the panicked, worried, or upset parts that are taking over their behavior. Their bodies are doing everything they can to regain a sense of emotional safety before the Broca's area enables them to describe their experience. On MRI scans of people exposed to trauma, the Broca's area seems to "go dark." In his book *The Body Keeps the Score*, Dr. Bessel van der Kolk calls this phenomenon "speechless terror."

That is not to say that every upset child is experiencing trauma. They're likely not. What is happening, however, is that this newly developed part of the brain is working hard to reconcile stress with the part of the brain that describes the experience. In other words, their limbic system and frontal lobes need to be working together for the child to be able to tell us what's up.

Otherwise, they can't tell us what's causing their distress. Once the limbic system and frontal lobes perceive a sense of safety and start communicating with each other again (subconsciously), the child will naturally use their words without being told to do so. Kids talk when they can!

Once again, with time and good ol' practice living life on Earth, kids' brains will grow and develop to help them communicate with us in more adultlike ways. Just like we can't make children's arms or legs grow faster, we can't make their brains develop faster, either. Only time and experience do that.

How nice it would be if a child's ability to regulate their actions and emotions were linear, but it simply isn't. The young brain is constantly forming and reinforcing (or breaking) neural pathways. These neural pathways are like little highways that tell the child where to go (or more specifically, what to do) when they encounter a situation. Unless they have practice "driving" a different way than they're used to, they'll keep driving down the same highway. The brain needs an incredible amount of practice getting things right and trying new roads, so to speak, before those connections consistently create mostly predictable results.

The good news about these neural pathways is that they're super flexible for kids. They don't need to spend a lot of time "un-training" themselves, because they have only so much life experience in the first place! Once they learn how to do something the "right" way, that habit is likely to stick until something else replaces it.

This is also great news for adults; we, too, can create new "highways" even if we've always responded the same way to a given stimulus (example: our child doesn't listen, so we yell). If we decide we want to handle things differently going forward, we can pave new roads and create new habits just by trying them out and keeping at them. Creating these new neural connections, which drive our new habits, is called *neuroplasticity*. The only difference between kids and adults here is that adults have to consciously decide they want to do things differently, and practice their new habits a bit more, for the neuroplasticity to work.

Think of it like this: perhaps every single day since you were two years old, you've put on your pants before you put on your shirt. Your default is going to be pants first every time. It feels right and natural to you to get dressed this way. However, if one day a law is passed that All Humans Must Get Dressed in Shirts Before Pants—even if you're open to obeying this law, out of habit, you might still grab your pants first for a while. But the more you put those pants back down and reach for the shirt instead, the easier it will be for you to eventually start with your shirt.

How would this translate for a behavior you'd like to change? Let's start with ourselves. Perhaps you've always been a yeller, and you want to stop yelling.

The key isn't to keep telling yourself to stop yelling. That would be like telling yourself, using the example above, to stop putting on your pants. Okay, but then what? We need to give our brains instructions about what to do instead. With what tool or skill do you want to replace the yelling? That's where your focus and practice need to be. I'll talk more about this later in the book.

To be fair, even adults well past the age of twenty-five vary in their abilities to handle different situations optimally and consistently. The variations adults experience in their own executive functioning skills depend on a whole host of contributing factors, such as emotional state, amount and quality of sleep,[16] activity levels,[17] gut health,[18] and more.

---

16 Jerrod Brown, PhD, "Executive Disfunction and Sleep Disturbances: A Brief Review for Professionals," Concordia St. Paul, February 4, 2021, https://www.csp.edu/publication/executive-dysfunction-and-sleep-disturbances-a-brief-review-for-professionals/

17 Yifan Zang et al. "How Does Exercise Improve Implicit Emotion Regulation Ability: Preliminary Evidence of Mind-Body Exercise Intervention Combined with Aerobic Jogging and Mindfulness-Based Yoga," Frontiers in Psychology, Frontiers, August 27, 2019, https://www.frontiersin.org/articles/10.3389/fpsyg.2019.01888/full.

18 Sung-Ha Lee et al, "Emotional Well-being and Gut Microbiome Profiles by Enterotype," Scientific Reports, Nature, November 26, 2020, https://www.nature.com/articles/s41598-020-77673-z.

Fortunately, parents can help children develop these skills and make the neural connections that make executive functioning, if not easier, perhaps a bit more consistent.

Story Teaching Is Part of Emotion Coaching and Executive Functioning

An emotionally regulated child is one who is ready to process new information, to see others' perspectives, and to grow their understanding of the world *and* of their own abilities. A child who's in a calm state is more likely to be able to feel empathy for others rather than be wrapped up in their own discomfort. As such, all these tools support healthy emotional regulation in children. This regulation makes them more receptive to story teaching.

As another sneak preview, here's the good news about story teaching: you don't have to be an endless fount of storytelling prowess. Just a few good stories that you can rotate will do just fine! More on that in the story teaching section (part 3).

Quick science tidbit: physiologically, although some children show signs of empathy as early as a few hours old (some babies cry when they hear another baby cry), the part of the brain that develops empathy largely starts to grow around age six or seven. It continues to develop through the teen years and beyond. It takes off around the middle teen years. If you're wondering why your younger child seems like they just don't care about others most of the time, it's because their brain literally hasn't grown enough to do that consistently yet.

Think of this information like the foundation for building a house. Without the foundation, the house can't stand. Similarly, story teaching works best when we've laid the groundwork by using peaceful discipline ahead of time. I'll cover how to do that in the next section.

Part 2:

HOW PEACEFUL DISCIPLINE WORKS

In this section, I'll cover how to help get your child into a place where they're able to learn from stories. In the meantime, if the child's behavior is suboptimal, or if they're in the middle of a big emotional release (which many think of as tantrums or melt-downs), *something* has to happen to ground them again before they'll listen to a single word we say. This part will cover that ever-elusive *something*. Essentially, this is a three-step process:

1. There's a triggering event; something goes wrong.
2. The child has an emotional release (or perhaps you do, which is also really common).
3. Finally, once things are calmer, you have a connection-and-teaching opportunity.

Kind of like in the classic board game where you can't pass "Go" and collect your $200 before you proceed, you must go through step 2 (handle the emotions) before you can move on to step 3 (teach). Otherwise, you're stuck. Unfortunately, as tricky as it can be, there's no skipping off the game board for step 2.

I'll also address how to stay calm in the moment, if you struggle with that. No judgment here—many of us find it incredibly difficult to be the proverbial calm in our child's emotional storm.

Fortunately, once we are emotionally regulated *alongside* our child, story teaching can happen. To reiterate, this section is about the in-between state—the bridge we can build to help move our child from tricky behavior to an "I'm ready to connect and learn" mindset.

CHAPTER 4:

HANDLING YOUR CHILD'S BIG FEELINGS IN A SUPPORTIVE WAY

This chapter addresses exactly that gray area where the child is *dysregulated* (struggling to find their calm), before they're ready to internalize any discipline (teaching) that would be beneficial to their optimal growth and development.

It's unlikely that a dysregulated child will be open to story teaching, or any kind of teaching at all, until they feel calm and emotionally secure again.

Often, adults are quick to want to "fix" children's feelings—to stop the crying, to calm the tantrum, to just make the discomfort stop somehow. Our desire usually comes from a place of great compassion and empathy, although it can also come from our *own* place of discomfort.

While our intentions are good, it's important to remember what happens when we stuff our feelings inside. We know very well what it's like when someone we love doesn't let us process our feelings fully. We feel unheard and invalidated.

As hard as it is, it's critical that we let our children get all their feelings out completely. This process is often referred to as *holding space* for feelings. In short, it means that more than just "allowing" feelings, we authentically welcome children to express themselves without judgment until they naturally find their way back to peace. It's an important part of the co-regulation process.

How Do We Hold Space for Our Children's Feelings?

I'm going to focus on what most people call tantrums since those tend to feel the messiest to navigate alongside our children. I prefer to call a tantrum an *emotional release*, because that's exactly what's happening—all those big feelings are coming out (albeit often like a freight train).

Why do I change the verbiage? I do it largely because it's helpful (and frankly, easier) to remember that emotional release is a healthy and beneficial process, and it has long-term protective benefits.[19] It's easier to have compassion and empathy when we think of someone expressing themselves versus thinking of that person throwing a tantrum. Equally concerning to me is *meltdown*. It connotes losing control rather than releasing pent-up stress.

Furthermore, we tend to think of tantrums as being limited to toddlers when, in reality, there are many versions of tantrums that aren't age-specific. Perhaps it's the older child who launches into a yelling tirade when they don't get their way; perhaps it's the tween who says unkind words and storms off.

Even adults sometimes have their own versions of tantrums. We slam doors. We yell when we don't mean to. We explode at those we love and say things we later regret about topics that may not even really warrant a big reaction. Just recently, a tired mama I know (ahem) complained about her daughter asking for a fourth glass of water right at bedtime. My poor kid was thirsty; mama's frustration didn't quench the thirst. I had to apologize for that one.

Everyone blows up or loses it sometimes. Those are all adult-size tantrums, and they have no expiration date until the adult

---

19 Lucy Cousins, "Can Always Staying Positive be Bad for Our Health?" Health Agenda, HCF, last modified August, 2022, https://www.hcf.com.au/health-agenda/body-mind/mental-health/downsides-to-always-being-positive.

finds healthier coping strategies. No one is perfect, and no one expects you to be perfect.

However, we can reframe the way we think about tantrums and rethink who we believe has them. When we do this, we're more likely to welcome big feelings when they come from those whose brains aren't yet capable of fully processing those big feelings, much less controlling their impulses.

Impulse control is part of executive function, which, as I mentioned, comes from a part of the brain that doesn't fully mature until around age twenty-five. If the child feels urgently compelled to scream, they simply *do*. It's loud, but it can also be quite developmentally appropriate. And yes, we can work with them to find other ways to express themselves.

Big Feelings: Babies and Toddlers

The first few years of a child's life are when their greatest brain growth happens—at times, as you recall from earlier in this book, they produce a million new neural connections per second! That's a lot of baby-size brain highways!

Young babies believe that they are literally part of their primary caregiver.[20] They have not yet developed a sense of their own identity. When they're upset, it's due to physical sensations or a need for emotional comfort; it is not due to something that would take a greater understanding of their place in the world to process. Regardless, their upsets are valid. Our best bet is to respond to them consistently and lovingly. Science proves that it's literally impossible to spoil a baby with affection and responsiveness.

Toddlers, however, gloriously and exuberantly know that they're their own people. They're very well aware that they have their own opinions, their own preferences, and their own ways of doing things. Accordingly, when a toddler has a big emotional

20 Illinois Early Learning Project, "Domain 1: Self Concept," University of Illinois at Urbana-Champaign (2022).

release about something, it may be due to physical sensations or the need for emotional comfort (just like a baby), but it also may be due to an understanding that something else is going on—something that's external to them and that affects them differently from how it would a baby.

A baby, for example, won't particularly care what clothes we dress them in as long as they're comfortable. A toddler, on the other hand, might care deeply that "today is a day for blue sparkles" and they'll let us know about it (even if they've never had a single blue sparkle in their wardrobe). Their emotional releases about these things are actually a sign that they're developing well. Their sense of self is solidifying.

We *want* our children to develop a sense of self, loud and messy as it may be sometimes.

Another good thing about these big emotional releases is that the child is learning that they have boundaries that are worth respecting. We want our children to have that perfectly healthy knowledge as they grow up. Toddlerhood is a wonderful time to develop an awareness of the value of self.

After all, we want our children to be able to stand up for themselves when they're older. We want them to manage the bully at school, the friend who wants them to try something they shouldn't, the unkind (or worse) boss or partner. We want our children to have practice asserting themselves to those people—and the only way they'll build that skill is by practicing it with us.

This can be a huge paradigm shift: we want our kids to practice pushing back on us. We're their best bet for teaching them how to do this safely and helping them learn that their voice matters.

Back to the incredible amount of brain growth that happens during these early years, we can see the importance of raising children with patience and a whole lot of grace as they navigate the incredible amount of information they're processing.

An Example:

One warm summer day when my child was two, I asked her if she wanted to go outside. She happily looked me square in the eye and replied, "Park! No pants!"

Oh. No pants, you say? I encouraged her to wear pants, but the more I persisted, the clearer it became that she was perfectly comfortable going without—and would not be persuaded otherwise.

We compromised. She went without pants, and I opted to keep mine on. Off to the park we went, happily as could be.

A helpful question for parents to ask themselves in the moment is "Will this matter down the road?" If not, you can likely let it go.

Big Feelings: Preschoolers and "Big Kids"

Older kids have big emotional releases, too. Although it's rare to see a nine-year-old splayed out on the floor, they're perfectly capable of door slamming, name-calling, yelling, and all sorts of other behaviors that can drive the most even-keeled parent to the other side of bonkers.

What then?

Their feelings are just as valid as anyone else's feelings, even if the way they express them sometimes leaves something to be desired. And just like everyone else, kids in this emotional state are not likely to want a story while they're overwhelmed and feeling dysregulated.

Good news: **co-regulation has no expiration date.**

The only difference is that, by now, children have more experience co-regulating with us, so they might want—or even need—some space from us before they want to be around us again for that beautiful co-regulation. This is actually a healthy thing developmentally, although it behooves us not to force it. Independence happens naturally when we've paved the way for it by making it emotionally safe to grow. And if the child still wants us to stay present, that's great!

My best advice is to check in and say what you observe: "I see you're feeling really upset right now. Do you want to spend some time together / need a hug, or do you need a few minutes to regroup? I'm here for you whenever you're ready."

By this age, kids are rarely shy about what their instincts are telling them they need. A slammed door is clear communication. Big tears and a near tackle of the parent to melt into their arms is communication, as well. If the child is waffling and sending mixed signals, staying close is usually best. That's fairly common for this age. Give them time and remain easily accessible. Sometimes, especially if their sense of self-worth is wobbly, they just need to double-check that the hug we're offering is really there.

In fact, when our kids push us away, say challenging things to us, or (even more frustrating) look at us and laugh when they've done something wrong, the behavior isn't usually intentional. Rather, it's a protective mechanism from the child's nervous system to help them regulate and repair with us (even if it doesn't feel like it). Think of it as nervous behavior asking for a hug. Even adults sometimes laugh when they feel uncomfortable.

Big feelings at this age can manifest in many different ways. However, your enduring presence and emotional safety are exactly what kids need most—even if how they express it changes like a yo-yo. All can be normal.

An Example:

One day when my child was four years old, we were running what should've been a quick errand through Target, an American big-box retail store that sells a little bit of almost everything. (Ha! Parents and our ideas of "should be.") My child was tired. My child was hungry. I thought, "Just this one more errand and we'll be done."

We'd gotten no farther than Aisle 2 when she saw a sewing machine for adults and announced, "Mama, we're buying this." I told her I didn't need a sewing machine. She looked at me and announced, "I do need it." I made the mistake of bluntly telling my hungry, tired four-year-old that indeed, she did not need a sewing machine.

Ever watched a space shuttle lift off? The people at the launch wear earplugs for a reason. My daughter's response offered a comparable sound in both volume and gusto.

I was caught entirely off guard; a foul mood was hardly ever one of her challenges. I froze. I tried to reason with her. (Ever tried to reason with the aforementioned rocket ship in the midst of blastoff?) I tried to move us to another aisle for distraction. Another bad idea.

After what felt like five thousand years (but was likely closer to two minutes), I decided to hold her. Just hold her. Validate her feelings. Support her (while praying that no one would come over the loudspeaker and announce, "Emotional cleanup in Aisle 2").

Rather than leaning out and trying to rush her through her feelings, I leaned in emotionally and just let her feel, telling her that I understood. You know what? It worked. Her anger turned to sadness, which turned to clinging and hugging, which turned to "Mama, can we leave?" We could. She clearly felt emotionally "done" in a good way. She'd gotten it all out, and we left with neither sewing machine nor shame.

Helpful questions for parents to ask in the moment: "What does my child need most right now? What would they find the most grounding?"

Big Feelings: Tweens and Above

Tweens and older children (aged twelve and up, approximately) are a special category insofar as their anterior insular cortex[21]—or, in words more of us can relate to, the specific part of their brain that handles empathy and decision-making—is better developed.

Still, development is never linear, so it's normal for them to sometimes behave like a younger child, and other times, possess all the innate wisdom of Rumi and Yoda combined.

By definition, this back-and-forth capability can feel exhausting for parents. Still, there's good news here:

- Co-regulation for the win! It really never gets old.
- Kids this age are self-aware enough that we can ask them what they need, and they usually know pretty clearly. Space? Connection? A few minutes to think about it?

The key words, if ever there were some for this age range, are "I'm here when you need me." That empowers the child to decide when, and if, they need our support. If we've co-regulated with them consistently up until this age, they likely have developed some of those ever-elusive and so-called self-soothing skills we covet for younger kids. They might be able to calm down and regulate on their own!

If not, they might still need a helping hand. That's perfectly all right. If they're feeling emotionally "small," they're still young enough that they might appreciate some genuine TLC from us.

21 Emily L. Dennis et al., "Development of insula connectivity between ages 12 and 30 revealed by high angular resolution diffusion imaging," Wiley Periodicals (2013).

We, in turn, can embrace these fleeting times, knowing that with every passing year, they'll likely be able to do more and more on their own—and need us less. Pass the tissues.

Still, it's hard sometimes.

No doubt about it: we're human. Having a child scream, flail, or rant in our general direction can feel off-putting, to say the least—especially if we were raised to "be quiet" or "be good" (whatever that meant), and full emotional expression was discouraged or disallowed. Of course, there was nothing wrong with expressing our feelings. Repressing feelings is an outdated and unhelpful idea that we can extinguish.

Sure, many adults were raised in emotionally healthy and nurturing homes. Others, however, were raised in a way that silenced our big emotions, leaving us unable to find healthy outlets for them. Many of us have repressed frustration, anger, rage, sadness, and a host of other feelings that can tend to cause not only physical problems as we age[22] but also rifts in our closest relationships.

We all know stuffing our feelings inside isn't healthy. Why would it be healthy for a child, then?

How much more beneficial it is to release those feelings than to carry them, repressed, into adulthood. The world doesn't need more angsty and disgruntled adults, that's for sure.

Still, we might feel some anxiety come up in our bodies when we are allowing our children to do that which we were not allowed to do ourselves, especially since science tells us that emotions actually are "contagious" (more on that in chapter 14).

In these moments, use your healthy coping tools to make peace with your own discomfort, be it through the proprioceptive tools I discussed previously or other actions that work well for you. You can create the kind of acceptance in your children's

---

22 Benjamin P. Chapman et al., "Emotion Suppression and Mortality Risk Over a 12-Year Follow-Up," *Journal of Psychosomatic Research* (October 2013).

childhood that you might not have had in your own.

Creating that acceptance can take a lot of self-reflection and a lot of internal work. It may require the support of a therapist or parent coach. No matter your preferred healing approach, it's very much worth the effort.

The result can be a happier, more grounded child—and, therefore, a happier and more grounded family.

What If We're Worried Our Child Is Really "Behind" Socially, Emotionally, or Otherwise?

I understand the natural concerns many parents have about their child's development and whether it's "normal," particularly if they suspect their child may have a neurological, genetic, and/or other developmental difference.

If you're concerned, investigate. Research child development online (from reputable sources) or from books, and if you're still worried, speak to an expert. A professional evaluation of your child can give you the information you're seeking.

The results of a professional assessment may confirm that your child is, indeed, right on track, even if they're different from their siblings or the kid next door. The range of "normal" is really quite wide. It's also really common for a child to be "ahead" in some areas but "behind" in others.

Why all the quotation marks? "Ahead" and "behind" and "normal" are often quite subjective. For example, at a play-based school, a young child who's wiggly and doesn't sit still much might be viewed as perfectly on track, whereas in a school with stringent academic focus, that same child may be perceived as having difficulties paying attention. Always consider the source if you're hearing concerns from others.

Knowing that there's a wide range of "normal" can help us, as parents, have a more spacious and curious mindset about where our kids really are holistically, rather than focusing on our child's perceived deficiencies.

An Example:

When my child was about six months old, her pediatrician asked if she was sitting on her own yet. She wasn't! I panicked. Catastrophizing, my mind took me to the worst-case scenario of her never being able to walk. I was sure there must be something terribly wrong.

After I thought about it, though, I realized that I loved carrying her and holding her so much that I'd actually never tried to sit her up! When we got home from the appointment, I promptly put her in the seated position on the floor to see what would happen.

Much to my surprise, she sat just fine for a good two minutes, her efforts only thwarted by our cat walking past and engaging her attention. The cat's ever-elusive tail was just out of reach, and stretching for it would be enough to make any six-month-old topple over.

Similarly, I had her evaluated again when she was two and a half years old, when she wasn't exactly thriving in her busy and noisy play-based toddler classroom. Long story short, there was nothing "wrong" with her. She was just an introvert whose sensory systems sometimes got overwhelmed with auditory input, especially having come from a very quiet home.

Sometimes things really do turn out fine.

Alternatively, you may learn from an evaluation that your child could benefit from additional support or resources. If that's the case, you're in good company! The sooner you know what's going on—if anything—the sooner you can seek the support your child may need. You haven't failed your child in any way, if that's your worry. Now you know, and you can do something about it.

Many kids are born with differences, and rather than focusing on where they're "behind," focus on how you can support helping them thrive *with* these differences. There are many versions of "fine," and "fine with differences" can absolutely be one of them. Play to their strengths and get help if you need it.

There are many great resources for more information about neurodiversity. You can work with your child's care provider(s) to see how story teaching may fit into the medical guidance you're receiving. All children benefit from respectful parenting, even if their individual communication style and/or day-to-day logistical needs may differ.

CHAPTER 5:

LETTING GO OF JUDGMENT

Just because we know tantrums can be a healthy release of stored emotion, that does not mean that they feel easy for us (or for the child who's in the midst of the emotional release). It does not mean that we always feel equipped when a child is splayed out on the floor at our feet—especially if we're in public or in another situation that feels particularly awkward.

Indeed, we often worry that we're being judged as parents. We worry that others are going to look at us and think, *I can't believe they're letting that child get away with that behavior.* Some adults even say that nonsense out loud, as if it's their business. We, too, may sometimes hear our inner voice communicating similar judgment.

Many people are unaware of the brain development that's happening during childhood; neuroscience is a modern advancement, and certainly not everyone is carrying around Dr. Dan Siegel's *Pocket Guide to Interpersonal Neurobiology* in their actual pocket. As such, many antiquated beliefs about how children "should" behave seem to permeate our culture, even when we have plenty of science to back up our knowledge to the contrary.

Simply put, we now know that kids should behave like kids (and that's a good thing). They are not mini-adults. Their behavior won't—and can't—reflect our nurtured and fully developed maturity.

The good news about judgment, however, is that *most* other parents aren't judging us condemningly. They're looking on with compassion and understanding our plight because they've been there. If they haven't, they can imagine it. They likely know that raising young humans isn't easy.

As for the few people who are looking on condescendingly, these are not the helpful or supportive people among us. It does not behoove us to take on their disapproval.

This is our relationship with our child, alone.

Moreover, we might be surprised to know that the sideways glances are often judgment of a different form. With the fortunate and continual expansion of positive and respectful parenting, other adults may be checking to see if the parent is showing up for their child emotionally and making sure the child is all right. That is its own brand of judgment, but it's helpful to remember that others might just be cheering us on when we support our children compassionately.

What About Our Own Judgment of Other Parents Who Aren't Being Gentle with Their Kids?

It serves us well, when we're tempted to judge other parents, to recall that we don't know what they're facing. We don't know the load they're carrying. We don't know the child. As hard as it can be, we can actively work to release judgment and simply do our part with our own children. And of course, *we* don't always get it "right"—which is all the more motivation to trust that we're seeing only a snippet of others' journeys.

An Example:

One day, I was in the checkout line of a store. (Yep. It was Target again. I'm wearing my mom badge as I write this.) Behind me was a mom with two small children who were acting like someone had fed them a hundred candy bars for breakfast. The kids were literally climbing the display shelves and trying to ride the conveyer belt toward the cashier. It wasn't pretty.

Unfortunately, the mom's behavior wasn't what I'd call "pretty," either. She was visibly livid, screaming at them, offering both bribes and punishments within the same breath. My stress level zoomed to near-maximum capacity simply sharing the space with them. I confess my mental dialogue started to turn judgmental. Knowing a thing or two about gentle parenting, I really wanted to "fix" it.

Catching myself, though, I paused and got curious. Eventually, I caught her glance. I smiled. She smiled a half-apologetic, half-exasperated smile back. I nodded and said plainly, "It's so hard sometimes, isn't it?"

She blinked. She blinked again. And then burst into tears. (Huh? I thought in a semi-panic.) She proceeded to tell me that she was a single mom and an elementary school teacher who was struggling to make ends meet—and that just two days prior, she'd been diagnosed with breast cancer.

After quickly and quietly berating myself for having judged that book by its cover, she and I spoke for quite a while. Before we parted ways, she said it had given her peace just to be able to speak freely to someone whom she knew she'd probably never see again, but who clearly cared.

That someone happened to be me, the woman who had just been judging her in the checkout line. I don't claim credit for having done anything good here, aside from being a vessel of the message to remember to give other humans a whole lot of grace. We really never know their stories. Compassion goes a long way.

The Importance of Looking Within

When our own inner judge is the one telling us that we're parenting "wrong" by "allowing" a tantrum, it sometimes helps to look within. Were we permitted to express ourselves freely and without judgment when we were little? Were we met with grace and emotional support, or something less comforting?

If we weren't met with full emotional safety from our own caregivers, this is a prime opportunity to break generational patterns. Once again, a trained coach or therapist can assist with this process if you need support. There are also some good books on re-parenting ourselves, such as *Parenting from the Inside Out* by Daniel J. Siegel, MD, and Mary Hartzell, MEd.

In the meantime, we can allow ourselves the grace to accept what we feel while we're healing, even if what we're feeling or healing is a long-standing or recurring emotional hurt.

Perhaps the most important takeaway here is that you, the parent of your own children, are empowered to choose your own way of parenting. You can release whatever is hindering you from having a true, deep, and rewarding connection with your family.

CHAPTER 6:

ADDRESSING PROBLEMATIC BEHAVIOR IN THE MOMENT

If someone's safety is at risk, or if some immediate damaging result of the child's behavior is imminent, then of course you should step in. Healthy boundaries are important.

Examples:

- If a child is actively engaged in harming someone or something, we wouldn't usually swoop in with a story to fix it. We can calmly and peacefully step in, cease the altercation, and remind our child what to do. Positive language works best for the dysregulated brain: "Hitting hurts; use gentle hands" is easier for a growing brain to process than "Stop hitting." The child's brain needs to know what to tell the hands *to* do, not just what they can't do.

- If a child is emptying the silverware from the drawer onto the kitchen floor, approach them confidently yet peacefully and remind them, "Silverware stays in the drawer to keep it clean."

It's important to add the *why* so your child understands the reason you're stopping their behavior. Otherwise, they may perceive it as adult control for no good reason.

One point of reflection about "no good reason": the child *always* has a reason, just like we do. It might be connection-seeking. It might be old-fashioned curiosity about how the laws of physics work in kid terms. (Example: "What happens when I push on this side of the plant with varying degrees of force?") When we hear ourselves say, "No good reason," that's a great time to get curious about the child's perspective, and not assume they have bad intentions.

Of course, you can remove the child from a situation if they're seemingly unable to cease what they're doing. A reaffirming "Looks like you're having trouble stopping, so let's move into the other room" can sometimes be enough to set things right again.

That said, there are times when story teaching in the moment actually works quite well!

Here's an example of a typical punitive response to the situation you'll recognize from chapter one::

A parent walks into their child's bedroom and finds the child, for no clear reason, pulling all the clothing out of the dresser drawers and throwing the items haphazardly across the floor.

Without missing a beat, the parent yells, "What are you doing? Stop it! Put these clothes away right this second! Sheesh—I just folded them! What are you trying to do to me?" The parent then storms out, warning the child they have five minutes to make the room spotless or there will be negative consequences.

The frustration is certainly justified. Who wants to put away laundry once, let alone twice?

At the same time, the child likely feels small after having been yelled at by their trusted big person. The child may or may not know why they were throwing the laundry. (Boredom? Curiosity? Temporary loss of marbles, literally or figuratively?) The child may also feel afraid; perhaps of the punishment itself, or perhaps of their perceived loss of connection with their parent.

Either way, the child feels distant, helpless, and small—and likely sad or resentful.

Soon thereafter, the parent may have collected themself and now feels like a jerk, having yelled for what feels like the hundredth time this week. They hate the way their outbursts seem to drive a wedge between them and their child, even when the feelings are justified. The guilt feels heavy and oppressive. They want a better path forward, but where to start? Is change even possible, much less a change to which the child will actually respond?

Nonpunitive version with an in-the-moment story:

A parent walks into their child's bedroom and finds the child, for no clear reason, pulling all the clothing out of the dresser drawers and throwing the items haphazardly across the floor.

The parent, noticing that this is unusual behavior for the child, gets curious about what's motivating them to make the mess. As the child grabs the next shirt from the drawer and it becomes airborne, the parent catches it midair and exclaims, "Interception! Number 38 catches the pass, makes a line drive down the field, and dives in for the touchdown!" (The adult may use the drawer where the shirt belongs as the end zone and return it to its proper place.)

American football fan or not, this will likely get the child's attention and interrupt their laser focus on messing up the room—at least long enough for the parent to stay in character and either:

- Calm down, go to the child lovingly and peacefully and ask what's up, or
- Invite the child into the story

If the adult chooses the latter, this can be extra helpful. After all, as Swiss psychologist and genetic epistemologist Jean Piaget noted, play is the language of childhood.

Where does it go from here? It depends on what's going on for the child. The child may divulge that they're trying to find their red socks / stuffed animal / whatever, in which case, the adult can say something like, "Okay, team. Let's come up with a plan. We're going to find your thing, and clothes need to stay in the drawer. Let's see how we can find it while keeping the clothes out of the lava on the floor. Quick, catch this sweater and toss it back in the drawer for the two points!"

Why, yes, I did just instantly transform the football field to lava, all while the adult stayed in character as "Number 38." Strange and wonderful things happen in the world of play. I intentionally included a rather ridiculous transition here to demonstrate that stories are flexible and open to whatever—truly whatever—works for you and your child, no matter how inane. In fact, the more inane, the better. Story teaching this way is memorable. Next time the child is tempted to launch the clothing, they're very likely to remember the whole lava situation.

Did you notice I also stated the boundary? "Clothes need to stay in the drawer." I didn't need to be heavy-handed to be clear.

Plus, last I checked, the floor becoming "lava" is almost universally enjoyable for kids, save for those sweet and sensitive souls who prefer to avoid uncomfortable concepts (and/or the young ones who may actually worry that the floor is becoming lava). Some children, especially little ones, can be very, very literal. That's normal.

As you can see, this story teaching didn't involve anything formal or planned. I call this *live story teaching*.

It looks a whole lot like a combination of improvisational comedy and playful parenting, where you and/or your child actually *become* characters, often unexpectedly. This crossover is intentional. Playful parenting is one of your greatest assets, and it works much better than directives, or just telling our kids what to do.

Why does live story teaching work better than directives? Can't we just tell our kid not to do whatever they're doing and make them remember?

Here's the funny thing about how brains work. We don't easily recall anything without some sort of anchor that makes it meaningful to us. A young child, naturally, won't care that rules are rules. That does not make them a bad human. It makes them . . . *human*. We need reasons to remember things; otherwise, our brains would simply be overloaded all the time. There's so very much to absorb from their environment at any given moment. (Remember all those new neural connections that are forming every second? It's exhausting for them!)

Science has our backs once again: the part of the brain called the *hippocampus* creates stories to help make sense of the events in our lives. We are quite literally wired for life through the lens of storytelling: "The hippocampus brings pieces of memories together over time and forms them into connective, narrative memories."[23]

Further, humans are wired by design to care about people more than things. It's how we stay alive from the very beginning. We're naturally geared for connection. If we can create mini-connections by personifying things, we help our children care about them more.

Even as an adult, if I'm worried about hurting a spoon by intentionally throwing it on the floor, I'm naturally wired to want to "protect" the spoon and keep it safe. (Yes, I know it's just a spoon, and no, I wouldn't do that—but many children would.)

Most importantly, whether you call it *playful parenting* or *live story teaching*, it's all about connection—100 percent of the time, connecting to people—connecting, I daresay, to the things we care about (even if they're just things).

---

23 Andrew Fell, "Hippocampus Is the Brain's Storyteller," Neuroscience News, September 29, 2021, https://neurosciencenews.com/hippocampus-narrative-memory-19383/.

Live story teaching helps foster cooperation naturally. It helps us connect and be close without power struggles.

Interestingly, unless the adult uses this approach too much—in which case it can be off-putting—there seems to be no upper age limit on when it stops working. The older the child, the less often you'll likely be able to use it. However, it's a fun tool to keep in your back pocket. Confession: I still effectively use versions of playful engagement with my husband sometimes.

For ages three to eight or so, however, play can be a common go-to and reliable support for you. You'll likely even see your child modeling it sometimes. That's when you really know your work in peaceful parenting is paying off!

One more note: in certain cases, some children (particularly those who are neurologically atypical) may benefit more from more direct (albeit still gentle and respectful) speech than they would from allegorical story teaching. Again, you know your child best, and you and your child's health-care provider(s) can explore how to support individual differences.

Seven Common Scenarios Where Live Story Teaching and Playful Parenting Can Work Wonders

A theme throughout is that the adult brings inanimate objects to life and creates "characters" of them.

Brushing Teeth

One fun way to accomplish this is to feign total incompetence. As you approach your child with her hairbrush, say (as if the hairbrush were saying it), "Ooooh, I've always wanted a turn at this! Time to brush your teeth!" Similarly, holding the toothbrush, say, "Oh, I will make your hair so fancy!"

Your child will love the feeling of power and total competence as they point out the error of your ways. The hairbrush and toothbrush, of course, will be shocked to learn their mistakes.

With exaggerated hesitation, they will agree to try it the child's way for a moment.

After a minute (especially if the child starts to protest), add, "That's right! I brush your arm! Arm, be still." Use it near your own arm if need be. It's okay to go back and forth a time or three to get it done. The point is to keep an unpleasant task more light-hearted.

Going potty

Try to trust your child's body and timing here. If they need help remembering to check, however, make it fun. Maybe, when they climb onto their toilet, they're climbing onto a choo choo train and one of you is the conductor. Or perhaps it's a rocket that's about to blast off to a new solar system. Bring that countdown to life before blastoff! For bonus points, the flush can sound the blastoff.

Putting on clothes

Role reversal for the characters can be really helpful, too. Do *you*, parent, fit into that 3T sweater—and perhaps you're asking your "Mommy" or "Daddy" or caregiver (a.k.a. the child) for help? Please try. Children love switching characters in life and taking on a role of authority.

If your child isn't keen to get dressed, a bit of laughter clears the air and helps you connect. It's worth the time to slow down and be silly if it cancels the forty-five-minute emotional release that might otherwise ensue.

Another great way to accomplish getting your child ready for the day is to involve the stuffed animals. They're your allies. Can your child dress a doll while you're putting on his socks? Can your kiddo tell you what his animal friend needs to wear for his rainy day, and what he might need to do to match him? Get your kids out of their heads here. Involve them in caretaking. Bring those animals to life. As you undoubtedly know, those babies are plenty real to your child!

Cleaning up toys

It's important to remember that once you have children, it's normal for your home not to look, well, anything like it used to. That's okay.

You might walk into a room and see a mess, but your child sees a world of possibilities. Allowing for some mess, even if only in certain places, might be one of the best gifts you can give yourself to reduce your stress levels.

When it does start to feel overwhelming, however, cease talking about cleaning and all that responsibility rubbish (child view). Your child will inevitably pick up on any anxiety you convey around cleaning. For everyone's sake, work to make it a peaceful and lighthearted process.

Since this is a common trouble spot, I'll share several ideas of how you can incorporate play and live story teaching into this sometimes-tricky topic.

The key idea is this: changing your nomenclature helps tremendously. Use kid terms. Not only enter but lead the world of make-believe.

When you see a bunch of toy cars all over the floor, notice the incredible traffic jam. The drivers need help getting back to their proper parking garage (the toy box). "Drive" them back together. Sound effects help—this story is actively unfolding before your child's eyes.

Building blocks have somehow scattered across the floor and need to make it back into the bag? No problem! You're not holding a bag, you're holding the hungry monster. "Feed me!" it bellows playfully. "Hungry! Must eat blocks! More! More!" On it goes until the mess is gone.

Even for adults, playing this way lightens our moods. Imagine what it does for our kiddos!

Get creative. If something doesn't have a logical home (like cars in a box you call a *parking garage*), make it silly. "Let's put all the dolls in the tree house (on the shelf) for the night!" Even a paper bag can be a tent for something. Bring toys and their storage spaces to life.

Last, remember how incompetent the hairbrush and toothbrush were at brushing teeth and hair? You're even worse when it comes to picking up the toys! A ball? It weighs as much as a semitruck! How in the world can you lift it? You are suddenly Weaky McWeakerson. Can someone save the day? (Many children love to rescue adults.) That giant toy elephant, however, is a breeze for you—it's light as a feather.

Your superpowers in live story teaching are very confusing—and hilarious.

Getting out the door

Although I often shy away from competition, this is the one time I'll offer a race. Which "race car" can put on shoes the fastest and touch the doorknob? Will it be Mama Racecar or Junior Racecar? For some kids (particularly highly sensitive children), however, competition can cause anxiety, so use it with caution. Also, letting the kids consistently win this race keeps it fun and engaging for them (although it's totally fine to have some very close calls). "Gentlechildren, start your engines . . ."

Likewise, who here is a bunny? Let's see those cottontails hop to the door. Prefer to be a human steamroller and roll across the rug to get there, flattening it on the way? Sometimes a different mode of transportation is all they need.

Supporting adults with day-to-day responsibilities

If your child can help put away non-breakable items from the dishwasher, for example, let them try. (Some breakable items are fine for some kids; you know your child best.) A great question to ask, even if they've done it before, is "Do you think you're strong enough to move these cups from the dishwasher to the counter?" Get them in character in superhero mode.

Children love feeling competent. So much of their existence includes not knowing what to do, so when they feel capable, it's incredibly empowering for them.

Encouraging positive behavior

If your child is struggling with a particular task that involves their body, for example, talk to the body part directly. Bring it to life as its own character. Let's say a child is handling the family dog too roughly. One option is to remind the child what to do in simple terms: "Gentle hands, please." This lighthearted and clear approach often works well.

A live story teaching modification would be "Excuse me, hands? Yes, all ten fingers—wiggle your way over here, please." Rather than looking your child in the eye, look at, speak to, and gently touch your child's hands as if they, alone, are the offending party.

This works particularly well for sensitive children who might feel embarrassed about what's transpired, or who have a tough time with correction.

You continue, "Dear hands, I could really use your help here. Our dog needs gentle hands only. Here are some things you can do. Would you rather have a hug, do some clapping, or wave yourselves up in the air?"

Live story teaching through play gets the "correction" done in a lighthearted yet effective way.

Most importantly, you can fold all these micro-stories, where you and your child have been in character, into longer teaching stories that you can use in both the proactive and retroactive models, helping avert or recover from similar tricky situations. Think of live story teaching as little snippets of what you can teach through stories to help reinforce the message. They're your cues/notes/outlines for the stories you'll tell later.

Live story teaching can work for other in-the-moment scenarios, too.

Let's take one more simple example. Let's pretend I have a beautiful flowering bush in my front yard. It irks me when my child pulls the flowers off and drops them on the ground. So, I try to make the bush a character—perhaps I name her Lilac—and say in front of my child, "Oh, Lilac! How lovely you look today! I love these flowers you've put in your hair. You must've worked all morning to make them bloom so!"

Here, when I see my child going for the first bloom, I can cut off her undesirable action at the pass with this simple intervention. Plus, because she has an anchor of personifying this bush, she's more likely to care about it than the empty words of "Don't pick the flowers." If she's very young (or older and missing the point), it's fine to add, "Let's leave your blooms right where they are today! [Child], let's show Lilac all the fingers that will not touch her today." Then, I remind my child what to do instead: "Here, fingers, hold this rake so we can make a big pile of leaves to jump in."

You may find this approach particularly helpful with those wonderfully sensitive children I mentioned earlier. They (we—hey, I was one of them) are much more likely to naturally care about inanimate objects than not. It's not weird; it's just that certain brains have been wired for a super-dose of empathy and compassion (increased neural activity in the areas of the brain that control feelings of empathy in sensitive individuals have been measured on fMRI scans).[24]

Finally, live story teaching can even work to support your child in their big feelings.

What if you created characters for emotions? To be clear, we have to be careful not to marginalize the child's experience or come across as patronizing. We can, however, label emotions and/or actions in supportive ways:

---

24 Bianca P. Acevedo, Elaine N. Aron, Arthur Aron, Matthew-Donald Sangster, Nancy Collins, and Lucy L. Brown, *Brain and Behavior*, Wiley Periodicals (July 2014).

- "Your Joy grew so big that you yelled with excitement and woke up your sister!"
- "Your Sadness wants to sit with us for a while. Hi, Sadness. You're welcome here. You're here to give us a message. Let's see if we can figure out what it is."
- "Your Anger made your feet start kicking again, didn't it? Feet, let's talk about some things you can do when you're mad. I remember how you can stomp around without hurting anyone. Let's be stomping mad together."

What if creating characters in the moment doesn't come naturally to us?

How does it work, though, for adults who aren't as naturally playful as kids are? Our brains are wired quite differently from theirs. As we know, kids can have fun playing with parents, friends, and even cardboard boxes. Not all of us have been to comedy school—do we have to be naturally funny or creative?

Not at all. In short, we can meet our kids where they are in their play. Join in and see what they're doing and wrap a story or a character around it. Opportunities often present themselves naturally if we enter our children's world of imagination. The great news for us is that if a child is already immersed in play, all we have to do is pay attention for a moment to see what natural "character" would go along with whatever they're doing. It's likely right in front of us.

An Example:

Let's say your child is busy playing castles and dragons / dress-up. However, it's time for dinner. Rather than making them disengage from their play, roll out an imaginary red carpet and escort Sir or Madam Hungrytummy to the table, arm in arm. Or climb into their invisible chariot that takes them to the banquet hall for the royal feast.

We don't need to manufacture something new and creative to make this approach work for our kids. We just need to let our guard down a bit and, to the extent that we can, see life through their lens for a little while.

Live story teaching is involved and connection-based parenting.

This is parenting for connection—parenting for the relationship not just for today but also for the long run. Sure, if you're new to creating characters in everyday scenarios, it might initially take you more time in the moment. Ultimately, however, it can spare your family bucketsful of tears and be entirely worth the effort.

Often, after some practice, cooperation happens so easily through play and stories that it's faster than any other alternative. Those extra minutes you invest now in learning these skills will ultimately save you gazillions of hours in struggles that simply won't happen anymore (not all of them, anyway).

As a side bonus, you might be surprised how self-sufficient children can become after they've learned how to do all these things in an emotionally safe place with you. Studies show that secure and healthy attachment, which are natural by-products of connection-based parenting, actually foster greater independence in the long run.

Live story teaching through play is a wonderful return on your investment. Long-term connection starts when kids are little, although it's never too late to start. It has a compounding effect—it grows over time, reduces conflict, and increases trust.

Being a playful parent who's willing to enter the child's world is a part of the equation that fosters connection for many years to come. It's all about the relationship.

Consent and bodily autonomy

I realize that some of you may be thinking, *This is all well and good, but what about the times my child digs in their heels in and simply refuses to do what I want them to do?* I get it, and I'd be remiss if I didn't touch on consent and the importance of bodily autonomy.

Bodily autonomy (the concept of being in charge of one's own body), related to consent (choosing to say yes or no to any activity), can be a tricky topic for parents.[25] We want our children to have healthy boundaries for their physical, emotional, and sexual safety. At the same time, we're their parents, and we have a responsibility to take care of them. What happens when our children say no to the care we're trying to provide? We want them to brush their teeth, right?

These suggestions can help you foster an environment of cooperation and mutual respect, while giving them an important sense of bodily autonomy.

Examine whether your nonnegotiable tasks are actually negotiable.

It's often helpful to investigate our motivation for those things we feel must happen. Sure, if you know that your children played in the dirt today, you might feel grossed out if they refuse their nightly bath. However, there's likely little risk that skipping the bath for a night (or more) will do any real harm. In fact, a little dirt might be good for their health.[26]

A bath might feel mandatory because it's what your routine has always been. Shifting routines can be jarring. Once you question your thinking, however, you might find more flexibility in whatever the issue seems to be.

If it's not really mandatory, let it go.

---

25 Sarah Aswell, "The Complete Guide to Teaching Kids Consent at Every Age," Healthline, last modified October 2, 2018, https://www.healthline.com/health/parenting/consent-at-every-age.

26 Lulu Garcia-Navarro, "Dirt Is Good: Why Kids Need Exposure to Germs," NPR News, July 16, 2017, https://www.npr.org/sections/health-shots/2017/07/16/537075018/dirt-is-good-why-kids-need-exposure-to-germs.

An Example:

Recently, my daughter fainted during a playdate at our local playground. Although everything turned out all right, it terrified me to have seen her unconscious so unexpectedly. I kept a close eye on her that day and made sure she received medical attention to rule out anything scary.

The next day, she was back to normal with a clean bill of health from her doctor. She was running around and playing as usual. At one point, she told me she was going upstairs to retrieve a toy.

Still feeling some anxiety, I said, "All right, let me hold on to your arm and walk up the stairs with you."

She asked why. I told her that because she had fainted the day before, I still wanted to stay close to her and help keep her safe, and how fainting on the stairs could be particularly dangerous. We briefly argued back and forth about whether I could go with her.

It was really important to me, and it felt mandatory in my mama heart. (Confession: this same mama heart had basically decided I wouldn't let her out of my sight until she was one hundred years old so that I could keep her safe forever.)

She looked me in the eye and said, "You realize that's your fear talking, right? I feel fine. You're an adult and you can work through your fear while I go upstairs and get my toy. I will be all right."

Oh, well, okay there, wise eight-year-old. She was completely right. It was my own fear and anxiety that made staying with her feel like a must. She really was fine.

Part of parenting is trusting our kids, even in situations like this one. If I'd made her accept my presence, what would that have done to her self-confidence? Her resilience? Her ability to trust that she can recover after scary things?

I breathed through my fear as I watched her ascend the stairs without incident, then descend a moment later with her toy in hand.

In trusting her, I proved to both of us that my mandatory thing truly wasn't mandatory. We both grew a little and came out stronger from my having backed away a bit.

Know which tasks aren't optional, and don't present them as if they are.

For *truly* mandatory activities that affect bodily autonomy, we sometimes apply the "ask for your children's consent" approach too liberally. If an activity related to bodily care isn't optional, don't present it as such.

Let's say, for example, that toothbrushing is a nonnegotiable task in your home. You might ask your child, "Can we brush your teeth?" If you inquire in that way, however, you're setting yourself up for a no-win situation if your child declines. Either you end up needing to force the action (that's not consent or bodily autonomy—forced compliance sends the wrong message) or you agree with their *no* and violate your own value around dental hygiene.

To be clear, I don't advocate forcing a toothbrush into a child's mouth. We do have flexibility on how and when the teeth get brushed.

Offering choices about caring for the body can help. You could say something like, "Would you like to brush your teeth before or after story time?" Or better, bring in a character for more live story teaching: "Do you want Mr. Bear to brush your teeth with his clumsy paws, or Hairy Fairy, who keeps thinking your toothbrush brushes hair?" It needs to happen, but there's flexibility in how it happens. Even better is involving the child in their own care. "Would you like the first turn?"

Alternatively, you could let your child know when it's almost time; a few minutes to mentally prepare is helpful. For children who are too young to have a good sense of minutes, frame it in understandable terms, such as, "After the amount of time it would take to watch one cartoon (be specific about one they can mentally reference), we'll brush your teeth." Then, proceed confidently and peacefully. Your vibe will set the stage for how your child responds.

Have a consistent routine and an "after plan" for these nonnegotiable tasks.

It lessens children's anxiety toward the dreaded activity if they know when to expect it. "Every day after breakfast, we brush, then we play." It's also helpful to have a consistently positive "after plan" (such as "then we play") sorted out so they don't fixate on the part they're dreading. Include them in deciding what to do afterward. Joint decision-making is part of bodily autonomy.

Since I'm on the topic, why not make that "after plan" five minutes of story time?

Try "I'll wait until you're ready."

"I'll wait until you're ready" is a powerful tool for consent. What might feel like no big deal to you might really be worrisome for your child. If you see any sign of greater-than-usual anxiety in your child's body (facial expressions, retreating, etc.), pause.

That doesn't mean your child gets to go play for three hours while you wait with the toothbrush in hand; it means you patiently wait alongside your child and co-regulate with them. Trust that your child needs a moment to adjust to whatever is about to transpire.

If he or she wants to go do other things, you can lovingly and firmly say, "Your game happens next; it's time to brush teeth first. I'll sit here with you until you're ready." Then, as hard as it is, don't pressure. Offer a hug or whatever calms your child. Sometimes, we all just need a moment to get in the right mindset. Maybe one or both of you needs a temporary change of scenery to recalibrate your nervous system and relax. Remember that you're united as a team here. Avoid power struggles.

Turn to more playful parenting techniques.

This is pretty much the golden approach to any tricky parenting situation, including bodily autonomy. Whenever you can, frame mandatory tasks as fun and positive. Give your child the first turn at washing their face, turn the bath into a splash party (after all, water is just water, right?), and try whatever else you can to ease the tension. We adults are often far too serious. Play is magical.

Another helpful option is the "Whatever you do . . ." game.

Here, you feign shock, horror, or disbelief as you tell your child, "We're going to play an opposites game. I'm going to pretend I don't want you to do something that I actually do want you to do. So, whatever you do, do *not* brush your teeth! Noooooo, not with toothpaste! Toothpaste is terrible!" Seeing a glimmer in your eye, your child will likely play along, happily "breaking the rules" of the horrible event you've jokingly forbidden.

Note that there's a difference between tricking your child and playing together. Games like this generally work best for children who are old enough for their sense of humor to have developed. Be totally transparent about your agenda. We don't send a positive message about bodily autonomy if we trick someone into compliance. In a game like this, you're united in the goal while they still feel protected and "in charge" of their body.

Give your children plenty of practice asserting their bodily autonomy.

Often, children are more reluctant to cooperate if they feel they haven't had enough say in their day.

Every child needs to feel he or she has a voice that matters, rights about their own body, and control over their health (even if they don't frame it that way yet). They need us to include them in their care. Some ways to give your child opportunities for consent about their body include:

Ask them overtly (with words) or silently through your body language, "Is it okay if I . . .

- Give you a hug?"
- Kiss your head?"
- Hold your hand?"

If they say no, you simply don't do it. It also means that when kids say things like this, you comply immediately unless it's a safety issue:

- "Stop tickling me!" (even if they're still laughing)
- "Put me down!"
- "Don't touch me!"

It also means that we don't play games like "You must pay the toll before you can leave my arms." (*Payment* is usually a hug or a kiss, which is the antithesis to bodily autonomy.) No child should learn that a forced physical act of affection (even in jest and not sexual) is payment for bodily freedom. We're planting dangerous seeds when we do that. The principle of consent related to their body doesn't disappear during games, regardless of who's playing it (parent, friend, or caregiver). Children must feel secure and protected in our care. Play is how they learn. They're learning about bodily autonomy and human rights with every interaction.

By respecting their bodies now, they learn the important principle that their bodies are worth respecting. We're the ones modeling whether their *no* has a voice in the world.

Most importantly, figure out the root cause of your child's hesitation to do whatever task feels daunting (or seemingly impossible).

Some truly nonnegotiable tasks, such as making a flight or an important event on time, might just need to happen. Support and validate your child's feelings, assure them that you hear their position, and move forward.

Revisit the conversation when you're in a good place to debrief. Assure children that you're a united front; you're on their side. Your child's well-being might take precedence over your punctuality. And sometimes, your child just needs you to listen without solving anything.

If you search your child's heart with compassion, you'll naturally align and connect about bodily autonomy / bodily consent and all sorts of other issues. From that alignment comes problem-solving.

For easier things like toothbrushing, you might learn that the water is usually too cold or too hot. (Or, as one little boy I know of complained, the water is "too wet." I wish them well with that one.) Many of what seem to be the biggest problems are easy to solve once you hear your child's perspective. Only good things can come from understanding our children's hearts.

With every interaction, you're laying the foundation for positive relationships with others as they grow.

And still, even with all this knowledge and these tools, we sometimes mess up and do things we regret as a parent. Been there. I get it. Fortunately, stories can help us repair and make amends, too.

An Example:

Recently, a friend called me in crisis. Although I'd been just about to start making dinner for my hungry and tired child, my friend asked if we could please come over right away.

I briefed my daughter on what was going on and asked, while I was shoving her coat over her shoulders, if she'd be willing to go with me in the car (I didn't have another great option for childcare right then).

My child very hesitantly said all right and put on her shoes at a snail's pace. As soon as we were in the car and driving toward my friend's house, however, she started lamenting the fact that we were going.

Surprised by her pushback now that we were already out the door and in a moving vehicle, I inquired, "You said you'd go with me, didn't you?"

She responded, "I said I *would* go with you, but I didn't say I *wanted* to go with you. I really don't want to do this. Can we please turn around and go home?"

Needless to say, this was awkward, because now my struggling friend was expecting us to arrive any moment. At the same time, my child made it clear that her *yes* wasn't really consent; it was forced agreement given the situation.

It was a good reminder to me to not only check in with my child's words but also to check in with her tone and overall demeanor. She's eight years old. She's still working on boundaries, and she wants to please her mama. It's on me to step back and look at the whole picture.

I don't want to raise a girl who says yes because she feels she must.

Looking back, I could've easily offered support to my friend over the phone. I could've paused and seen the big picture: a tired and hungry child in front of me, or a friend (who also has other friends besides me) across town, and who was not in such an extreme crisis that it had to be me or nothing, right this second. My superhero cape that displayed my "amazing friend" skills had blown over my head and blocked my ability to see what my child was needing. I had work to do.

Live Story Teaching for Repair

Live story teaching also works well when we've messed up (because we all mess up sometimes).

How this works is that we can give ourselves a character for those parts of ourselves that sometimes come out unwittingly. To be clear, these characters aren't an excuse; they don't help us pass the blame. To the contrary, they personify the parts of ourselves that we're working to modify.

"Name it to frame it" comes from the wisdom of Drs. Daniel J. Siegel and Tina Payne Bryson. While the good people who coined the term didn't literally mean "name it," I'm daring to go there. The gist of "name it to frame it" is that when we name our emotions, it helps us find peace with them. I'll expand on their concept a bit more later.

Here are some examples of how we can literally name the things we want to tame within our parenting:

- Adult speaking aloud to himself and with his child listening nearby: "Eek! Yelly Yellerson just showed up and got loud again, didn't he? Yelly, I hear you felt frustrated, but please go back down the kitchen disposal where you belong. I choose to be peaceful." (You might go turn on the disposal for a moment to emphasize your point.)
- Adult, also aloud: "Oh my. Dingleberry Guilt Trip just used some shaming words. No one likes being made to feel wrong. Dingleberry, let's give you another chance to try that again more peacefully."

Does it feel silly to refer to parts of your behavior in the third person? Perhaps. However, it gets kids' attention and can help diffuse uncomfortable situations while still acknowledging what in your own behavior went sideways. It's helpful to name the proverbial elephant in the room.

If this isn't your style, though, don't do it. What matters most is that you model authenticity. A sincere apology can be plenty. I'll cover apologies in a moment.

As a reminder, if you've messed up some parenting moments, you're human! Be kind to yourself. We all have tough moments/days/weeks.

You'll notice an important distinction in the types of names I've suggested: these were playful and brief descriptions of the action we took, not a judgment of our character. Yelly Yellerson clearly describes yelling. Dingleberry Guilt Trip describes someone who's indulged in a guilt trip. These are things we've done, not judgments about who we are.

I wouldn't use "Mean Daddy" or "Terrible Ted" or "Rotten Ramona" because mean, terrible, and rotten are all character judgments. We don't want to model for kids that we get to call ourselves names that label us negatively beyond the action we took. Labels stick, right?

In doing this exercise, we also model for children that they get to judge their own behavior separately from who they believe themselves to be. It's okay (healthy, even!) for a child to be able to acknowledge that they *made* a mistake. We do not want them to think that they *are* a mistake.

Finally, did you notice that in the examples above, the characters modeled a path forward? Being peaceful and getting a second chance are both admirable next steps. We can show our kids that even after big mess-ups, they can recover and course-correct.

All these examples work best, of course, when they're accompanied by a sincere apology. We don't want to blame parts of ourselves as a way to shirk responsibility for our actions. Modeling accountability for our mistakes is an incredibly powerful teacher—in doing this, we show our children that it's safe to get things wrong: to fess up, and to make amends with those we've hurt.

What does a sincere apology look like?

Sincere Apologies

I use a modified version of the work of the Gottman Institute:

1. Acknowledge that you hurt the child's feelings. ("I know I made you really sad when I yelled at you this morning.")
2. Apologize sincerely and ask forgiveness, without expecting anything—including forgiveness—in return. ("I'm so sorry I yelled. I was wrong to express my anger in such a harsh way.")

3. Describe the specifics of what you'll do differently next time (not just "I won't yell anymore," but something like "Next time I'm tempted to yell, I'm going to pause and take some belly breaths before reacting. You deserve to be treated gently and respectfully. Will you please forgive me?")

Some children—in their wonderfully brutal honesty—will say what many of us are thinking when we've been wronged: *No! I'm not forgiving you.* That doesn't mean you need to say or do more, nor does it mean they are guaranteed to never forgive you. Most of the time, it translates to "I'm still upset."

What we can do if this happens is to allow space for their feelings. We can't make them forgive us, but we can show them that it's safe to be upset. We love them, anyway. Period. Unconditionally.

What I've said when I've been in this situation—and believe me, I've been there—is simply, "I love you no matter what. I'm here for you when you're ready to reconnect or if you'd like to keep talking about this."

Time alone doesn't heal all wounds, but time and acceptance of what *is* (rather than forcing what we wish were the case), do. Part of live story teaching is allowing whatever needs to unfold to do so in its own natural time. We can remain available to our child, not withdrawing but allowing them time to process as they may need to.

According to relationship researcher and expert Dr. John Gottman, it takes approximately five positive interactions with someone after a rupture to fully heal the connection.[27] That doesn't mean you need to go out and buy your child five presents or do five of anything. What it means is that your child needs to feel emotional safety and connection approximately five times

---

27 Shruti S. Poulsen, "A Fine Balance: The Magic Ratio to a Healthy Relationship," Purdue University, March 6, 2008, https://mdc.itap.purdue.edu/item.asp?itemID=20410.

before they can truly let bygones be bygones. It's just the way humans are wired. It's how we rebuild trust.

In the meantime, we can hold ourselves with self-compassion and grace. Dr. Mona Delahooke describes this poignantly in *Brain-Body Parenting*: "For now, if you are blaming yourself for negative interactions you've had with your child, know that children take in the aggregate of all our interactions. When we show up and repair as necessary, we help our children develop confidence in the world and in themselves."

Part of ongoing repair with our children, and ourselves, requires that we have a coherent narrative about our experiences together. I'll cover how that works in part 5, "Stories for Healing."

Live Story Teaching—Should We Name the Child's Character?

You might be wondering if we should use a character to describe, or personify, our child's tricky behavior. In general, the answer is no.

Here's why: no one likes having their own behavior labeled by someone else. You run the risk of hurting your child's feelings on top of the dysregulation that caused their suboptimal behavior in the first place.

Plus, only the child knows what's going on for them beneath the surface. If we say, even in jest, "Hey, is Bossy Billy coming out again?" Billy might have a legitimate hurt underneath the surface that caused him to act that way, and now he's being called a name.

Even though you're calling the behavior a name (and not the child), children—and, heck, some adults—have trouble discerning between calling their behavior a name and believing it's a character judgment.

> Example: Let's say a child is repeatedly taking another child's toys. If the adult comes over and says, "That's mean," the child may perceive it as if the adult

> had said, "You're mean." Of course, that's unlikely to be what the adult intended, but the child still internalizes the hurtful words. Try a gentler and more neutral approach, such as saying, "Those toys belong to x. I'm curious what you like about them." Then, work with the child to find a mutually agreeable solution.

Once again, you can model how to do it safely and effectively for yourself, but it would be unreasonable to expect a young and developing brain to comprehend the difference if they're already struggling.

It is true, however, that sometimes a child's behavior simply warrants some action in the moment, and we may feel this way especially if we're feeling triggered. I'll talk more about this in chapter 10, where I cover the HUG process.

In the meantime, though, we'll cover some things to think about as they relate to common consequences of a child's behavior. With curiosity and an open mind, we'll explore calm-down corners, time-outs, time-ins, and other consequences.

CHAPTER 7:

RETHINKING CALM-DOWN CORNERS, TIME-OUTS, TIME-INS, AND OTHER CONSEQUENCES

Many of us were raised with punishments for the infractions we committed. Some of us go on to justify those punishments by saying things like, "I *deserved* to be punished when I was bad. If I'm speeding on the highway and I get pulled over, getting a ticket is my punishment. Punishments *work*."

Let me ask you this: When you see those flashing lights in your rearview mirror, what feelings course through your body? For me, it's two things: 1) some level of terror, and 2) immediate shame. Although I've been pulled over for speeding only once in my life so far (knock on wood), I still have visceral memories of how awful it felt.

Yes, punishment teaches, and I'll expand on that in a moment. Here's the thing, though: if we want a connection-based relationship with our kids, we can't expect them to feel connected *and* meet their struggles with the parental equivalent of a speeding ticket from a (rightfully or wrongly) angry police officer every time they misstep. Our children generally aren't engaging in behaviors that have the potential ramifications that a car accident could. They're kids. They're doing the best they can with the skills they can access in the moment.

As for kids "deserving" punishments, it's interesting to note that children believe they deserve whatever treatment we give them—not because of what they've *done* but because of who they *are*. Children often believe that good things happen to good people, and bad things happen to bad people. That's how it works in the movies they watch, right? The good characters are rewarded, and the bad ones are punished or permanently exiled. No one goes after the bad characters to remind them they're still lovable. Therefore, if something bad happens to a child (a punishment), they may think it's because *they* are bad and not worthy of acceptance. We do not want children to carry this belief about their inherent self-worth into adolescence and adulthood.

Note how different this message is from "Everyone makes mistakes and I'm here to help." Scaring, shaming, or making kids feel awful should not be our starting point when we find children doing something they shouldn't.

What if we start with compassion instead? What if we look at the root causes of the behavior rather than punishing only what we see on the surface?

Yes, it's a paradigm shift for a lot of us. It shakes our internal script about how we do things.

If you're willing, let's unpack the highway-speeding example a bit more. For starters, I don't have a long-term relationship with the police officer who pulled me over, so there's no opportunity for connection or repair. Second, I'm an adult who truly does know better than to put others' lives at risk by speeding. The onus was on me to have been paying closer attention to my velocity. I messed up, and I'm willing to own that.

Just like I naturally wanted to do well for this officer and to keep others alive on the highway, our kids naturally want to do well for us, too. They inherently want our approval.

Plus, when it comes to our children, we're going to keep living with them—so connection and repair *are* part of our relationship. We will share the same space, and we both want to feel good about that.

In summary, it's all about our intent, and more importantly—the child's perception of that intent. If we want a peaceful relationship, including *correcting* our children peacefully, we need to be peaceful. It starts and ends with us. We're the only ones in charge of our part of the dynamic.

When your positive intention and your child's perception of your intention are in line with one another, odds are good that you're parenting peacefully.

If harsh punishment through yelling, shaming, or other adult-imposed consequences aren't the answer, what about lesser consequences? Let's examine a couple of common approaches.

"Calm-down corners" or time-outs are a common form of consequence. Do these help kids to regulate before story teaching? Certain forms of non-punitive time-outs are helpful. For example, some children do well with sensory and/or comfort items when they're upset, and their adults create special spaces uniquely designed to hold these items for their child. These kids may also thrive in having a quiet space of their own, especially if they're sensitive to the noise and chaos of a busy day. It's important to differentiate between disguising a "time-out," when intended to be punitive and cause distress for the child, from a sacred, peaceful place that is truly comforting.

When used punitively, consistently sending the child away to process their big feelings or "think about what they've done wrong" sends the child the message that our love and support are conditional, and that only certain feelings are safe to express with us. Kids rarely think about what they've done wrong while they're in a punitive time-out. Instead, they're usually either hurting (guilt or shame) or angry (feeling wrongly accused and/or resentful).

This approach does not make their feelings go away, nor does a magical time-out fairy appear in their time-out corner and coach them through how to behave better next time. Instead, it teaches them that our love is dependent on their behavior, and they come out with no greater skill set than they had previously.

They learn that if they act a certain way, we find them acceptable; if not, we don't, and they feel they're no longer worthy of our love. They don't learn to come to us when they're struggling; they learn to retreat from us.

In extreme cases, regular experience of being sent away can be processed as emotional neglect, which risks setting children up to develop coping mechanisms[28] that may not be healthy as they continue to grow. They may learn to withdraw or bury themselves in unhealthy habits that seemingly take away the pain at times when they desperately need help. We want them to feel safe to come to us as they get older and face bigger challenges.

This does not mean that all their behavior is acceptable. What it means is that we accept their *feelings* and we give them tools to help them when they're struggling. I'll discuss this shortly.

In positive discipline, we remove from our vernacular statements like "Go to your room and come back when you're ready to behave / be calm / talk nicely again." Instead, we welcome the child in our space no matter how they're feeling.

Uh-oh moment: You might be thinking, *Eek. I've been using time-outs for discipline because I thought they were fine.* You're definitely not alone here, and they certainly do improve upon many of the alternatives they were designed to replace, such as corporal punishment. We all work with the best option we know at the time. If this is still where you are and it is progress from where you've been before, take a breath and give yourself lots of grace.

Furthermore, I've never met a parent who didn't sometimes just need some space. Right. This. Second. If you're in that place emotionally, I hear you. As we parent our children, we're in a constant state of learning and stretching and growing. I'll share some ideas about parenting time-outs in a bit.

If you do opt for a "calm down" area, I recommend keeping it somewhere close to you, or better, staying with the child. This teaches them that we're an emotionally safe place for them to

28 M. J. Lawler and E. B. Talbot, "Emotional Neglect," *Developmental-Behavioral Pediatrics, Fourth Edition* (2009).

share their feelings. With this approach, we set the stage for ongoing trust and open communication.

We're planting seeds about whether they feel they can come to us unconditionally. Naturally, we want to be a safe haven for them. This doesn't come out of nowhere. They learn to trust in our emotional availability when they're young—and it's not just from our saying, "You can always come to me no matter what." Our responsibility is to follow through.

We want to be the kind of parents to whom our children run, rather than from whom they retreat, when they're hurting. When we are peaceful, it becomes clear to children that although we do have boundaries that we'll uphold when necessary, all their feelings are safe with us. What an important distinction to learn!

Time-In: The Peaceful Alternative

When we use a time-in instead of a punitive time-out, it creates a natural state of bonding and connection. Kids like bonding and connection, and so do we. It sets us both up for success.

How it works is that we simply choose to do something unrelated to the problem at hand. It doesn't mean we're sweeping the problem under the rug. To the contrary, we're calling it out in plain sight while also showing our child that our relationship matters more than any problem we face together.

We can say something like, "I'm uncomfortable with the way you spoke to me a few minutes ago, and we'll address it shortly. First, let's calm down together for a little while. We'll solve the problem best when we're both feeling peaceful."

From there, we go and "do our thing" (co-regulate) together. Consistency often works well, and we can customize it to our child's personality. Here are some commonly used options that work well and enable you to see the problem with fresh eyes:

- Read a book together to get our minds off the stressful situation.

- Gently roughhouse (important note about tickling: some kids' stress levels decrease with tickling, while others' increase, so make sure to get their consent). Some fun and safe physicality can help reduce the tension between you.
- Invite the child to sit on your lap and ask them to draw a picture of how they were feeling at the time of the conflict.
- Take a short walk together. Nature is incredibly healing.
- Have a dance party with big, unpredictable, chaotic movements before returning to calmer ones; move that energy!

What doesn't usually work as well is to go "have a time-in" in our own separate spaces; once again, co-regulation is at the heart of connection. It's all about feeling emotionally safe *together*.

Once everyone's regulated again, we can address the problem through a lens of curiosity, cooperation, and peacefulness. We can brainstorm together because we're coming from a place of mutual calm rather than chaos.

But doesn't it work when we punish kids by isolating them?

That depends whether you're looking at the short term or the long term. Short-term behavior modification systems, including those that promote isolation in a punitive way, can indeed "motivate" the child to comply.

We're not looking for short-term wins, however. This is fear-based and control-based parenting. Rather than driving kids to "obey," it actually drives children to simply hide their behavior from us. They just get better at not getting caught so that they avoid punishment.

Furthermore, isolation-based strategies can damage their trust in us. These strategies don't promote respect; if anything, they damage it. We can unwittingly send our child the message "My parent can't handle me." That's a lot of responsibility for a child to bear!

With this in mind, we remember that children are not just "little adults." There are better ways to address misbehavior without isolating them.

What should parents do, though, when their kids' behavior requires a response of some sort, and they want to address their children using nonpunitive, positive discipline?

The solution often rests in natural and logical consequences.

What are Natural and Logical Consequences, and How Do They Work Within the Boundaries We Establish?

What natural consequences and logical consequences have in common is that they peacefully teach children their so-called life lessons. That's the essence of peaceful discipline: teaching that does no harm.

When used correctly, natural and logical consequences are valuable teaching tools.

An important distinction to make, of course, is to know that both natural and logical consequences are different from boundaries. Boundaries are the loving and fair guidelines that help ensure children's safety, health, and social-emotional growth.

Ideally, when the child is old enough, most boundaries can be co-created between the adult and child. To do this, both parties brainstorm together, are careful not to criticize each other's ideas, and continue until they mutually agree on workable plans.

Boundaries that adults and children co-create are more likely to work than unilaterally imposed boundaries that come only from the adult.

Why is this?

Children naturally feel valued, just like adults do, when they've had a vote in how their life is run. The same psychology is at work when citizens in a country vote for the country's leader who they believe will be fair and just. No one wants a dictatorship.

An Example:

Recently, my daughter had a mess on the floor behind her dollhouse. She was happy with her setup, but I grew concerned that it would become a breeding ground for who-knows-what.

Dictator Mommy (me) showed up and told her plainly to clean it up. That plan didn't fly.

Peaceful Mommy (also me) got the hint and decided to overthrow Dictator Mommy. Using one of her dolls (Queen Mouse) as my helper, I humbly requested of the queen that my daughter and I be allowed to tidy up her courtyard. "Speaking" through my daughter, Queen Mouse responded, "Yes, you may, but only after lunch and after we get my valuables out of the way."

This was a reasonable trade for me. I could wait until after lunch, and since my daughter (through her stuffed animal) suggested the timing and part of the process, she had already "bought in" when it was time to follow through.

Dictator Mommy would've made a bigger emotional mess of that small physical mess, and probably would've ended up with a sad little girl. Instead, with a co-created boundary and follow-through, we kept our afternoon peaceful and positive. Phew! Close call.

How soon can we start co-creating boundaries together? Very soon! You can ask a toddler whether they want their bath before or after their nap, for example. If your toddler doesn't like choices yet (for some, it overwhelms them with too much "power"), try again in the preschool years.

This doesn't mean you have to make everything a choice; that could be overwhelming to anyone. Some people suggest choosing low-stakes items (the bath time I mentioned) for starters. For older kids, it's perfectly helpful to give them high-stakes decisions, such as, "Hmmm. Phones are expensive, and I didn't plan on getting you one until a few years from now. Do you want to wait until I can get it for you as I planned, or do you want to get a part-time job to save up for it yourself?" For the latter example, if the child says they'll get a job but they quit after two weeks, the boundary might be that you're not getting them the phone yet.

To be clear, some boundaries should be adult-directed. For example, a parent gets to keep their preschooler safe by saying no when the child wants to turn the knobs on the stove. This parent also gets to say no when their middle- or high schooler wants to go to a party where illegal substances may be available. There are many examples of boundaries that adults should set; I recommend being clear on the *why* so that children understand the purpose of the boundaries.

What about when the child crosses those boundaries, though?

Natural and logical consequences are incredible teachers. They're not punishments; they simply occur as the effects of choices. Think of consequences as nonpunitive teachers.

Consequences can be positive or negative. For example, the consequence of a child treating a sibling well is usually a peaceful relationship. The consequence of a child mistreating a sibling is usually conflict.

The place where boundaries and consequences meet is often where learning happens best.

A natural consequence is a "cause and effect" relationship that is directly related to the child's behavior.

> Example: A child says he doesn't care that he's left his favorite toy truck outside in the driveway. The parent warns the child that the toy might break or be stolen if he leaves it there overnight. Still, the child refuses to retrieve it.

Sure enough, the next morning, the parent backs out of the garage to take the child to school and has completely forgotten about the toy truck. The car rolls over the truck, and they hear the dreaded crunch.

The natural consequence is that no one can fix the truck and the child is sad.

The broken truck and the sadness of the child are enough of a teacher that the child doesn't need further punishment for having left the truck outside. The natural consequence here is plenty.

The likely result is that next time, when the adult says to the child, "Please move your toys off the driveway," the child will be more inclined to remember the broken truck and consider his options more carefully. If he chooses to move his toys, that will result in a positive natural consequence—nothing breaks. He'll learn greater responsibility naturally.

Logical consequences are consequences that are a related and connected progression of the situation that's already in motion.

Just like natural consequences, logical consequences are not punishment. Still, they're very effective teachers.

Example: A child who struggles with screen time wants to keep playing her online game even though she's exceeded the daily screen limit to which she and her parents had previously agreed. Perhaps she's sneaking away from the dinner table to check in under the guise of going to the restroom, or she's feigning sleep and staying up late chatting online with friends.

Her parents are aware of what she's doing, yet they know punishment will only make her want to hide her behavior further. Resultantly, her family wants solutions that help their child feel seen and validated, while still holding the agreed-upon boundary.

Although natural consequences might include letting her stay online and face the repercussions of being overtired at school the next day, her mom and dad realize that logical consequences might be in order. It's not that logical consequences are harsher or better teachers but, rather that there might be safety or logistical reasons that she shouldn't be exhausted at school. Maybe she's a new driver and needs to be especially alert.

Logical consequences might include allowing her to use the device at will or within specified windows, and asking that she give it to her parents for safekeeping at a mutually agreed-upon time.

Likely result: she'll find a way to balance her time more effectively.

As an aside, another important option worth considering is to see if it's time to revisit her daily screen limit. Perhaps the limit wasn't realistic and genuinely warrants another look.

Although natural and logical consequences are not punishments, children might still have big feelings about them.

It's normal and developmentally healthy for children to question and push back on boundaries, especially those where they didn't have any input. In fact, it behooves adults to let children practice pushing back. It's much safer for a child to practice boundary-pushing with a trusted adult than with peers, for example. In many cases, negotiation is a positive.

Still, children might have big feelings when grown-ups stand firm on healthy boundaries. If the boundaries are reasonable and fair, the parent can uphold them confidently and with compassion. At the same time, if the consequences make sense to the child, there may be no pushback at all!

An Example:

One late afternoon, I took my daughter ice skating in our neighbor's backyard (they're avid hockey players, so they freeze their entire yard every winter). My daughter is brand new to skating and loves it.

We'd been skating for a while that day, and as time really does fly when you're having fun, I lost track of how long we'd been there. I realized that we'd significantly encroached on dinnertime and needed to get home to cook right away if we wanted bedtime to happen at a reasonable hour.

Better would've been to give my daughter plenty of notice and agree on a stop time, but I'd already dropped that ball (or in this case, puck). I told her we had to leave right away. Understandably, she didn't want to stop so suddenly.

Realizing that I'd been unfair about it and not wanting things to escalate further (and hence, delay us longer), I told her she could have ten more laps around and then we'd go. We did the ten together, but then she still wasn't ready to stop.

I held firm on the limit. She pushed back. Quickly, it turned into a tug-of-war, and I wasn't being the gentle parent I strive to be. My anxiety was talking. I finally convinced her to go to the side of the rink and started helping her toward the exit.

We stopped for a moment so she could regain her balance on the ice. She looked at me very seriously and said, "Stop pulling me!"

I replied, "I'm not pulling you. I'm just holding your arm to help you balance."

She responded, "No, I'm not talking about that. You're pulling me emotionally, and I don't like it."

Oof. She was completely right. No one likes being coerced

or forced or made to do something against their will. I realized that I was being a big walking, talking stress ball and I was co-escalating (heightening our collective stress rather than co-regulating), thereby making the transition harder for her. If I wanted to change the trajectory of this exchange, and likely the mood of our entire evening, I needed to do something.

So, I paused. I took some calming breaths and stopped rushing her literally and emotionally. I apologized for the abrupt change. I co-regulated with her and kept the tone light by asking, "I'm curious what would help this transition be easier for you."

She replied, "I still don't want to go, but you could be a whole lot more playful about leaving."

Ah, right! Play! Of course! (True. She shouldn't have had to remind me, but I hadn't completely regained my peaceful parenting wits yet.)

I invited her to skate on an imaginary tightrope with me all the way off the ice. She willingly complied, and we went home to dinner happily and without stress.

The natural consequence, which I didn't even need to mention, is that we had a little less time than usual before bed. The night proceeded smoothly.

Sometimes, natural consequences work best. Other times, logical consequences are the way to go. When we're wondering which to use, we can check *our* intent to make sure both options are peaceful. If not, keep brainstorming alternatives, ideally with your child. Consequences are not designed to be punitive or to create emotional distance. The goal is to find a win-win.

Gentle, respectful parenting isn't boundary-less parenting.

Limits can and should be loving. Ideally, the parent will have collaborated with the child to find mutually agreeable behavior *before* a situation has escalated.

The key to this peaceful approach, of course, is being proactive. In the example of the toy truck, the parent might've used play to engage the child in collaborative problem-solving rather than only leaning on a factual warning that something might damage the truck.

Lighthearted and playful parenting removes the vast majority of potential conflict.

When I recently shared the ice skating example with a parenting group I'm teaching, one of my students asked me, "What if she'd continued ice skating without your permission?"

Great question.

My answer was that if I'd forced her to stop "because I said so," the situation would've morphed into control- and behavior-based parenting, rather than connection-based parenting. Sure, I'd have been frustrated if she'd done that. When I stop myself and ask, "What's the end goal I'm trying to accomplish?" my answer is to get us home peacefully.

Yelling at her or punishing her would not be peaceful. My job, then, is to behave in a way that encourages her to feel connected, because when kids feel connected, they *want* to do well for their special big people. I am 100 percent confident that connection is what worked on the ice rink that day, and neither of us had to suffer for it.

And yes, if she'd continued skating without me, we'd have had a problem-solving discussion about that later, once we were both regulated again. She'd only have kept skating if she had felt dysregulated and emotionally disconnected; I'm confident of that. Connection begets connection; punishments beget pain and further dysregulation.

With All This Talk of Punishments, What's Really Wrong with Them, Anyway?

A parenting approach that focuses too much on parental control and punishment is often called *authoritarian parenting*. It's linked to a host of problems as the child grows older. Here's what research from Michigan State University tells us:

> The negative side effects to [authoritarian "control- and punishment-based"] parenting include: Children are aggressive, but can also be socially inept . . . Children in these families have poor self-esteem, are poor judges of character and will rebel against authority figures when they are older. Children will model the behavior shown to them by their parents while with their peers and as future parents themselves. Children rarely learn to think on their own. Children have a difficult time managing their anger and are very resentful.[29]

True, not all punitive parenting comes from authoritarian parenting. It's a very common combination, however. Both are the manifestation of an adult exercising control over a child. What's the child to learn in that?

Adult-driven punishments don't help children internalize the intended message—and they often backfire.

If a child feels the parent's punitive "teaching" did nothing more than hurt their feelings and/or the relationship, the adult-driven consequence is not likely to be an effective teacher. It only teaches the child that the adult has control over them. The consequence does not get to the root cause of the problem.

Continuing the ice skating example, if my child had kept skating and I'd punished her by taking away a privilege (let's say device time), that's not a natural or logical consequence. The only possible result would have been my child feeling angry and disconnected from me. She might comply the next time, but it would be based on fear and resentment, and it would do no favors for our end goal: a healthy, loving relationship.

---

29 Tracy Trautner, "Authoritarian Parenting Style," MSU Extension, Michigan State University, January 19, 2017, https://www.canr.msu.edu/news/authoritarian_parenting_style.

If anything, when it comes to most punishments, some children will learn to hide their misbehavior better due to fear of being caught, rather than change their actions. According to the Society for Research in Child Development, punishing children for lying actually makes them *more* likely to continue lying:

> [Researchers] compared the lie-telling behavior of 3- and 4-year-old West African children . . . from either a punitive or a non-punitive school. Children were told not to peek at a toy when left alone in a room. Most children could not resist the temptation and peeked at the toy. When the experimenter asked them if they had peeked, the majority of the punitive school peekers lied about peeking at the toy while significantly fewer non-punitive school children did so. The punitive school children were better able to maintain their deception than non-punitive school children when answering follow-up questions. Thus, a punitive environment not only fosters increased dishonesty but also children's abilities to lie to conceal their transgressions.[30]

Many punishments don't account for where children are in their development.

Even if they can walk, talk, and tie their own shoes, children are not miniature adults and can't be expected to act as such. They may sometimes exhibit emotional maturity to make grown-ups believe their brains are working like adults' do, but that's simply not the case.

As I've mentioned, until that prefrontal cortex is more fully developed (around age twenty-five), the child's brain simply won't work like an adult's does—because it *can't*.

As evidence of this, rather than fending for themselves, chil-

30 Victoria Talwar and Kang Lee, "A Punitive Environment Fosters Children's Dishonesty: A Natural Experiment," Society for Research in Child Development, October 24, 2011, https://srcd.onlinelibrary.wiley.com/doi/10.1111/j.1467-8624.2011.01663.

dren often act in ways that seem to be attention-seeking, when really what they're seeking is *connection* to someone they hold dear. More on this shortly.

Furthermore, sometimes they'll act with empathy and seem to convey a deep understanding of others' perspectives, while other times, they'll seem selfish.

As it turns out, this "focus on the self" (egocentrism) is exactly what helped increase a child's odds of survival from an evolutionary perspective. Not that long ago, children literally needed adults to focus on them so that if, for example, the mastodon were charging them, they'd get the adult to whisk them away to safety. They couldn't have done it alone. Today, being focused on the self is a healthy and normal stage of growing up.

Science reminds us that kids' brains aren't designed to take on others' perspectives consistently or treat others "fairly" yet:

> Egocentric behavior in children may not be a function of an inability to know "fair" from "unfair," but is instead due to an immature prefrontal cortex that does not support altruistic behavior when faced with a situation that has a strong self-serving incentive.[31]

We can't make kids grow up faster, but we can support optimal brain development and gently help nurture emotional intelligence.

Learning about child development can help grown-ups manage their expectations about what's normal, and parent accordingly.

Let's explore the perception of attention-seeking behavior a bit more.

Many parents hear at some point—often when they have newly emerging toddlers, but certainly much later as well—that their

31 "Self-centered Kids? Blame their Immature Brains," Science Daily, March 7, 2012, https://www.sciencedaily.com/releases/2012/03/120307132206.htm.

children's troubling behavior is simply attention-seeking. Further, parents hear that the best thing to do is simply ignore the attention-seeking behavior and it will naturally stop on its own.

There are some flaws to this parenting advice, however. It's true that attention-seeking behavior isn't always pleasant. That said, we need to explore what happens when we ignore it—especially when parents perceive the advice to ignore the attention-seeking behavior as meaning to ignore the child (often isolating the child in time-out or otherwise). We also need to know what to do instead.

Some people perceive these activities, among others, as attention-seeking behaviors:

- Seemingly doing things the child knows are off-limits, or doing things we think the child should know better than to do
- Pushing boundaries
- Whining
- Crying for what we perceive to be no good reason
- Acting out

But are they really attention-seeking behaviors? It may help to reframe them. If a child is seeking attention, no matter the form, it's because they're craving connection with their trusted adult. Attention-seeking is attachment-seeking.

Although attention-seeking behavior in adults can be problematic, it's completely developmentally normal and healthy for a child to crave attention from their caregivers. Their brain may be so dysregulated from anxiety or other factors that they're unsure how to connect in a positive way. As a result, they grasp for whatever works. These attention-seeking behaviors certainly do get our attention.

Such behaviors are not a reflection of how "good" or "bad" a child is, however. Rather, they're a reflection of what behavior their brain is capable of manifesting in any given moment. Using the examples above, a child doing these things is likely longing to be "seen." Ignoring a child who feels this way would only exacerbate the problem.

Here are three things that happen when we ignore attention-seeking behavior:

1. We send the message to our kids that our love is conditional.
2. We miss an opportunity to help our kids' brains grow.
3. We miss the opportunity to address the underlying need.

In more detail:

When we ignore attention-seeking behavior, it sends the message to our kids that our love is conditional.

Just like it can be confusing for an adult whose partner is giving him or her the so-called silent treatment, it's even more baffling for children when we simply don't respond to whatever they're doing. What they know is what they observe: "My trusted adult isn't seeing me. I've disappeared from their world." This perception may lead to feelings of isolation.

According to experts, the risk factors of feeling socially isolated are multifold, such as:

> poorer overall cognitive performance, faster cognitive decline, poorer executive functioning, more negativity and depressive cognition, heightened sensitivity to social threats, a confirmatory bias in social cognition that is self-protective and paradoxically self-defeating, heightened anthropomorphism, and contagion that threatens social cohesion.[32]

While ignoring a child might "work" in some sense (they may stop performing the undesirable attention-seeking behavior), it can come at a very high cost.

---

32 John T. Cacioppo and Louise C. Hawkley, "Perceived Social Isolation and Cognition," *Trends in Cognitive Science* (August 2009).

What should we do instead?

As Daniel J. Siegel, MD, and Tina Payne Bryson, PhD, explain in *The Power of Showing Up*, one of the tenets of secure attachment in a child is feeling fully "seen." To do that, we need to acknowledge whatever our child is doing and address it accordingly.

Helpful reminder: Connect before you correct. (This is a common peaceful discipline quote commonly attributed to Dr. Laura Markham.)

A child often isn't mentally capable of hearing instruction or correction when he or she is acting out. The part of the brain that handles those types of conversations is essentially in an off position until a calmer state of being is regained.

Therefore, it behooves the adult to understand this and wait out the storm: stay present with the child physically and emotionally, and ensure safety for everyone involved. If the child will let you, you can hold them, invite them to your lap for a story, or find another calming activity to help regulate their brain (by which I mean, to turn the rational part back on). This may take a while—that's okay. Let the emotions flow as much as they need to without invalidating the child's feelings or experience.

As soon as it's appropriate and still top of mind, the adult should describe what they've seen: "You didn't like when I said it was time to put away your toy cars, so you threw them all on the floor." Keep judgment out of it; state only the irrefutable facts.

From there, the adult can remember that it's not an adult-versus-child situation. It's both parties working to solve whatever the problem is. The child is not the problem; the behavior is. In this example, it might look like: "We need to keep the floor clean so no one falls and gets hurt. Let's drive your cars back to their parking lot and keep everyone safe."

For a child who's emotionally grounded again by this point, playful parenting can prove immensely beneficial to accomplish whatever task needs to be completed. Further, it helps the child feel "seen" and empowered to be part of the family again rather than ostracized from it. If the child isn't yet emotionally grounded, we keep co-regulating until they are.

Most importantly, this connection-based approach to attention-seeking behavior shows them that our love is unconditional. That's the most critical message they can possibly absorb.

When we ignore attention-seeking behavior, we miss an opportunity to help our kids' brains grow.

If an adult physically and/or emotionally ignores a child who's struggling, the child has no model of how to better handle whatever tricky situation they're experiencing:

> When risk factors are present, and they are not mitigated by some protective factors, children are more openly negative in their expressive behavior.[33]

This translates to a snowball effect. A child who's behaving poorly is more likely to keep behaving poorly rather than learn an alternative more positive way to behave. What should we do, then?

We can model emotional regulation, rather than matching our child's upset with our own. And instead of leaving the child to figure things out without help, we can model that it's okay to have feelings and express them peacefully. We do this knowing, of course, that children are, by definition, less mature than we are.

When a child is engaging in attention-seeking behavior, we can help them cope by modeling a more appropriate way to manage their big feelings. We can help retrain their brains to understand that when they do an undesirable behavior, they can come to us for support rather than waiting for our disappearance or punishment. Canadian psychologist Donald Hebb, and more recently, Dr. Dan Siegel, remind us, "Neurons that fire together, wire together." In other words, repeated exposure to a new way of thinking trains their brains so that this new way becomes the default way to respond.

---

33 Pamela M. Cole and Amber E. Jacobs, "From Children's Expressive Control to Emotion Regulation: Looking Back, Looking Ahead," *European Journal of Developmental Psychology* (February 2018).

In learning to trust that we're an emotional safe haven for them, they can start to depend on us more consistently, and come to us proactively when they're struggling, rather than acting out to get our attention.

Children are only likely to persist in attention-seeking behaviors if we're highly inconsistent in our response or unclear about what a better alternative is. A caregiver who sometimes isolates or ignores the child, but other times is gentle and nurturing, would send a very confusing message to the child. It is better to reliably provide a how-to manual for the child's emotional responses by giving clear and age-appropriate directions.

Further, we can (and should) set healthy boundaries about what is and isn't acceptable behavior. What's more important for a child to know than "I can't do x" is "I can't do x, *but I can do y*." If we consistently remind them of what the boundary is *and* what the better solution is, that knowledge can create new pathways in the brain.

When we ignore attention-seeking behavior, we miss the opportunity to address the underlying need.

Experts agree that all behavior is communication. Even when we don't like the way a child is expressing what he or she wants, the underlying need that they're trying to convey doesn't magically go away if we ignore it. Perhaps the child is hungry or tired, or over- or under-stimulated. Or perhaps we've been on our phone too much and the child is lonely (I've been guilty of this more times than I'd care to admit). Maybe they're simply seeking connection. (This is often the case.) The child might not even know why they're acting the way they are, but they're still looking to their trusted adult to help them work through their big feelings.

What should we do instead?

If we can solve the attention-seeking behavior with a hug, that's usually an easy fix. A snack? Doable, although we should be wary of solving problems by offering food every time. Some downtime or a game together? Sure. Whatever it is, if we can find the root cause, it's much more effective to address it than to pretend it's not there. In the latter scenario, we risk sending the message to our child that their needs don't matter.

Helpful reminder: Needs are needs are needs.

Just like we did when our children were babies, it's helpful to have a mental (or even a physical) checklist to review:

- Is my child too hot? Too cold?
- Hungry?
- Tired?
- Sick?
- Bored?
- Needing gentle physical connection?
- Craving downtime with less noise?

We sometimes assume that just because kids are older, we can throw away the old checklist. In truth, though, it's as valid as it ever was.

What's the bottom line on how we should handle attention-seeking behavior?

One of the most important things we can do is know what's developmentally appropriate for our child. It's a wonderful investment of your time to study this, not only for your child's sake but also for your understanding of how to parent appropriately. A key takeaway is that play will continue to be your child's primary language for many of their formative years. Even more than that, it's critical that we know our own child, even more than what the parenting books or experts say our child "should" be doing. We know our kids best.

Once again, we need to reframe attention-seeking behavior from having a negative connotation to a developmental expectation that we have of our children. Of course they need our attention. They're children. What they want more than anything is to rely on our acceptance, our unconditional love, and our (fairly) consistent emotional presence.

Most punishments are strategies to gain compliance rather than foster connection, but we pay a steep price for the long-term results.

If an adult thinks connection is *not* an appropriate way to teach, these counterpoints are worth considering:

- Do grown-ups learn best when someone approaches them in anger or peace?
- Do grown-ups learn best when their feelings are validated or when their feelings are pushed aside?

Further, when children grow older and need to navigate friendships, relationships with teachers and other students if they go to school, and eventually in the workplace, will their parents have modeled how to address conflict peacefully or through force? What about intimate relationships?

Kids are no different from grown-ups in these respects. Grown-ups can effectively teach responsibility, how to learn from mistakes, and other important lessons using nonpunitive strategies. Causing emotional or physical pain to teach simply isn't helpful.

What about strong-willed children? Don't they need harsher lessons to make them learn?

A so-called strong-willed child is often named as such because of power struggles with the parent. Indeed, kids who seem to be especially stubborn can legitimately be frustrating for their grown-ups!

Interestingly, when kids are strong-willed, many adults respond by digging in their heels and attempting to make their children less strong-willed. From the child's perspective, however, the grown-up is just as strong-willed as they are.

That's the classic recipe for a power struggle.

The remedy is *not* to be stronger than the child in an eternal tug-of-war until the parent wins but rather to teach in ways that have only positive consequences.

Oftentimes, if a child is strong-willed, the solution is to find a new way to communicate with that child. Natural and logical consequences can be particularly effective teachers for these kids. And bonus: they're often much less work for the grown-up!

> Example: Sometimes grown-ups get stuck in a sub-optimal discipline pattern, such as yelling. If yelling isn't working, the child doesn't need the grown-up to yell even louder. Volume isn't the issue. Perhaps slowing down and peacefully getting on the child's level would get the child's attention better. If a solution isn't working, it's not the right solution.

Why Some of the Most Commonly Used "Consequences" Don't Work Long-Term

Below are some drawbacks of common punitive approaches.

Removing a toy, privilege, or device time is not a natural or logical consequence.

Unless the toy, privilege, or device is directly the source of the child's problematic behavior, removing these items only teaches the child that the adult has the power to control them.

In the earlier examples of natural and logical consequences, taking away cartoons, for instance, from the child who left his truck outside, would not be an effective teacher.

This punishment is not related to the child's ability to understand the repercussions of his actions. It's like telling a child who's been eating apples that he can't have oranges anymore.

A punitive time-out is not a natural or logical consequence.

As discussed earlier, sending a child away to process their feelings or "think about what they've done" rarely results in a child actually thinking about what they've done. More likely, they feel emotionally unsupported and unsure of what to do in the future when the triggering situation comes up again. It's as if they're given a destination with no map of how to reach it.

Indeed, there's a big difference between a punitive time-out and a calm-down corner for co-regulation. One is helpful for teaching, the other drives emotional distance.

Spanking/smacking is not a natural or logical consequence.

Spanking is associated with a host of significant problems, both short-term and long-term, for the child's development. Although some parents claim it's a good teacher and is helpful for changing behavior, those changes in the child's behavior come from fear.

Even if the parent spanks only after their anger has passed, or makes it what they perceive to be a mild spanking, a child's nervous system is incapable of telling the difference.

Spanking a young child breaks trust and may hinder development in the same ways that even stronger forms of abuse do. Further, spanking may even contribute to long-term behavioral and mental health problems.[34]

Spanking increases the following:

- Potential for increased aggressive behavior; child aggression may increase and endure into adulthood.[a] Further, corporal punishment to "fix" children's aggressive behavior may actually exacerbate physical aggression continually. Adult aggression is not the antidote to child aggression; it only fuels it.

- Negative developmental outcomes, including lower IQ.[b]

---

34 University of New Hampshire, "Children Who are Spanked Have Lower IQs, New Research Finds," ScienceDaily (September 2009)

a https://www.ncbi.nlm.nih.gov/pmc/articles/PMC3768154/

b https://www.webmd.com/parenting/news/20090924/kids-who-get-spanked-may-have-lower-iqs#:~:text=In%20one%20study%2C%20researchers%20analyzed,as%20a%20form%20of%20discipline.

- Continuation of family violence being passed down from generation to generation, creating a deep trauma history and increased risk of psychiatric disorders.[c]
- Greater likelihood of future substance abuse (alcohol and street drugs), as well as greater risk for suicide.[d]
- Increased risk factor for anxiety disorders and antisocial behavior.[e]

This is hardly a win.

Threats, bribes, and rewards are not natural or logical consequences—nor effective motivators—in the long run.

Bribes and rewards are problematic in their own right. If used excessively, they can result in a child who complies only when bribed or rewarded, thereby damaging their intrinsic motivation.

It's understandable. Even adults learn quite quickly to hold out for the prize. It's not manipulation; it's human nature.

Threats are, like punishments, a component of fear-based parenting. No one wants a relationship based on fear of what might be taken away, up to and including a parent's affection.

Even smaller and seemingly more benign threats, such as "If you don't go to bed now, you won't get to watch your favorite show tomorrow," can create anxiety. Without the right support, anxiety-ridden children often grow into anxiety-ridden grown-ups.

In this bedtime example, a better alternative would be "It's time to sleep. I want to make sure you feel rested and happy tomorrow. Let's get cozy and relax together." The focus is on what the child gains, not on what they risk losing. Again, the grown-up can uphold the limit with compassion and empathy.

That said, I am not completely opposed to the occasional "carrot." It's fun to have something to look forward to. For me,

---

c https://www.ncbi.nlm.nih.gov/pmc/articles/PMC3447048/

d https://www.ncbi.nlm.nih.gov/pmc/articles/PMC7983058/

e https://www.apa.org/monitor/2012/04/spanking#:~:text=Many%20studies%20have%20shown%20that,mental%20health%20problems%20for%20children.

as an adult, it might be some good food when I'm done writing today, but it's more likely to be reading a library book or the green light to do something I've been wanting to do. The difference is that the thing I get after completing my tasks doesn't really influence my motivation to do them—it's just something to look forward to when I'm done. I think of it more as a celebration than a reward. I don't overuse it.

Some people will say, "That makes no sense! Even adults work for the paycheck. The paycheck is the reward." I hear that argument, and I ask in return, "Are you working only for the paycheck?" Sometimes, yes. Ideally, however, we find jobs we also enjoy just for the sake of doing them (and the paycheck is the proverbial icing on the cake). The paycheck is a necessity, but the intrinsic motivation that's much more meaningful is feeling like we're contributing to something greater than ourselves. We want to like showing up for work each day.

To use an example for childhood, let's say you're wanting to encourage your little one to use the toilet instead of diapers, so you reward them with a sticker every time they make it to the loo. Is your goal to have them develop a lifelong passion for stickers, or to not have to call you to the restroom to help them when they're thirty-five years old? Using the toilet on their own is a life skill they can be proud of no matter how old they are! They don't need stickers to learn this skill. The intrinsic motivation of knowing how to use the restroom successfully is reward enough.

Which are better, natural or logical consequences?

To be clear, both natural and logical consequences are better than punitive discipline. Both can address misbehavior in ways that help children learn how to get along well in the world. Additionally, natural and logical consequences can be inherently positive experiences for kids.

Children can learn responsibility and self-discipline without being punished. The normal effects of living life and learning from experiences can be wonderful teachers.

CHAPTER 8:

NEGOTIATING FOR THE WIN-WIN

A lot of people think positive parenting and peaceful discipline mean giving children everything they ask for (i.e., permissive parenting). As my child will readily tell you, there are plenty of limits in our house.

During my long stint in corporate America, I took an executive negotiation class that completely changed my perspective on *no*. Although it wasn't intended as such, it's been one of the best parenting skills I've ever learned.

As odd as it sounds, the most successful *no* often sounds surprisingly positive. Encouraging, even.

Who'd have thought executive negotiation tactics would double as positive parenting tools? Before anyone worries that I'm suggesting children should negotiate everything with their parents, I'm not. We still get to have boundaries. I strongly believe, however, that the words we use with our children become their inner dialogue as they grow up. Perhaps even more important (and less clichéd) than that idea is that the emotional tone we set becomes the emotional tone they'll have on their own.

Both our verbal messages and our tone stick with them. I see evidence of that in my own child in the ways she matures and processes various situations. The world will give her plenty of *no* (heck, it already does), so I choose to teach her optimism and hope as tools for resiliency. And more than that, there's plenty of Internet-searchable evidence that authoritarian, my-way-or-the-highway parenting causes substantially more harm than good. I've touched on some of that earlier in this book.

Here are some ways to express a positive emotional tone with your kids:

1. Skip the battle.

If you know you're going to a store that has things your child will ask for but you're not planning to buy them today, offer a pre-emptive alternative. Different from a "negative no," which might sound like this, "We're going to the store now, but you're not getting anything," spin it a different way.

Try, "We're going to the store now. If you see something you like while we're there, remind me to take a picture of it. We'll put it on your list."

Helpful hint: Building your child's trust that something is actually going on their list might not happen overnight. When you do buy something for them later, it helps to verbally add something like, "I remembered that time we went shopping and you put it on your list. That's how I knew you'd like it." Reinforce that you've paid attention.

You can also be clear that putting something on the list does not always mean they should expect to receive it later. Getting comfortable with the "maybe" can help build their executive function skills, this time, in the form of delayed gratification.

2. Offer some control.

People (big and little) often feel the most defensive and dig in their heels when they feel they have no control over a situation.

When it's time to get out of the pool, off the swings, or whatever, we can't spring the news on them and expect immediate compliance. Fair warning helps everyone involved. It would be like having your friend or partner walk up to you, snatch your phone from your hand, and say, "You're done with that now!" It wouldn't go over well, would it? We all want some notice when something's going to change, especially if we're enjoying it.

That said, for a child who can't tell time, "We're leaving in five minutes" would be meaningless, but it can be helpful for older kids. If your child wants to keep doing what he's doing but your answer is no, reduce your child's resistance by trying this: "It's almost time to go. You pick a number (or give a range you can manage, especially if your child knows lots of numbers). I'll count to that number while you finish what you're doing, and then we'll go. What number would you like?"

For what seemed like forever, the highest number my child knew was thirty-one. Counting to her biggest number helped her feel like we were staying for the maximum amount of time in her universe of numbers, and the glimmer in her eyes as I counted proved how she loved having that influence on our day.

3. Agree for a future date.

Sometimes, there really isn't a way to accommodate your child's request when they want something. That's fine. Give them peace of mind by telling them that a version of their request will happen instead.

Example: If your child wants chocolate chips on their French toast, try this: "Chocolate chips really are delicious! Although I'm not putting them on your breakfast this morning, how about if we plan to make that pumpkin chocolate chip bread you like next weekend?"

Again, the part you own is making good on the alternative you've suggested. Build trust that you'll follow through. If they want to go somewhere you can't go right now, intentionally let them watch you put it on the calendar for a day you can go.

There's a world of difference for a child between hearing you say, "Sure, another time," which he likely translates as "Probably never," and "Yes, let's put it on the calendar together. Come look with me for our first available day." Apply this to little things while you're building trust in this area. Nothing is too small when it's important to your child.

As an aside, I did once agree to my child's request for chocolate chips on French toast, and I have to say, it was delicious.

4. Reframe the *no*.

Sometimes when I'm tired or impatient, I hear myself bark, "No, stop that!" What I fail to teach in those moments, though, is *why* it's important for my child to change course.

An Example:

One night recently, my daughter was pulling repeatedly on the cord for the window blinds, making them go up and down, up and down. The cord was snapping back on the blinds and making them wind up too tightly. In my desire to have her stop immediately, I yelled at her to knock it off.

She kept on pulling, pausing only to ask why.

From her perspective, she was doing nothing wrong. We open and close the blinds every day. She added, "I'm trying to figure out how they work inside the part we can't see."

Ah, right. My little scientist. Naturally, she'd want to know why, and since we're not a "Do it because I said so" family, her desire to continue made sense. Only after I explained that pulling the blinds up too tightly could break them, and *why* it could break them, did it make sense to her to stop. She willingly let go, with remorse for having potentially damaged them.

Unless it's an urgent safety issue, find a positive way to redirect your child. Little and big kids need this. A better option for a little kid might sound like, "That's the floor. Let's find some paper for you to color on instead." For a bigger kid, try, "Hmmm, it's getting close to dinnertime, so let's stay inside now and make a plan to go back out tomorrow."

I hear myself saying, "Let's make a plan . . ." a lot when the timing or approach my child is using isn't workable for me. Choose your words to encourage rather than discourage.

Note that in all these examples, there's no unreasonable negotiating, no cajoling, and no bribing: we're shopping, but not buying what you want today; you need to stop doing what you're doing; we're not having chocolate chips today. A *yes* that you can offer might include:

- "Yes, we can do that tomorrow."
- "We're all done with it for today, so let's make a plan to do it again in the morning."
- "Let's wave at the playground as we walk past it today and tell it we'll see it on Thursday!"
- "Yes, the next time we're at the store, you can pick some out."

An important note about the topics that are urgent safety issues:

Some parents refute this kind of parenting with statements like "Well, if my kid is running toward the street, I don't want to teach them to turn around and negotiate with me! When I say stop, they have to listen the very first time!"

I hear you. I, too, raised a toddler with legs. Here are a few ways to handle situations like those:

- Practice using a code word, such as *freeze*. Play the "freeze game" ad nauseam until your child masters it. Practice indoors and outdoors. Freeze while dancing and running, and so on—whatever makes it second nature to them to freeze when they hear the word. If you see them running toward the street and you yell, "Freeze!" they'll have practice knowing what to do.

- Stay close to your child when you're in potentially dangerous situations. Kids have impulses. Our job is to protect them as much as we can.

- Know that, in many cases, even young children can tell the difference in our tone when we're playing versus when we're being serious.

5. Find something on which you *can* agree.

When all else fails, in executive negotiation terms, find your BANTA (Best Alternative to a Negotiated Agreement). BANTA means that even if you can't reach an agreement (in this case, with your child), you can still find something to agree on, even if it's agreeing that it's hard to not get what one wants. Sometimes, no just needs to be no.

Offer empathy while your child emotionally processes the limit. It's normal for a child to get upset at *no*. (We all do!) And you don't need to fix it. Help them understand that you're on their side even when you disagree. Feel their perspective; internalize it.

Sit quietly with them while they express their disappointment, just listening and understanding, without justifying or defending your position. Hold space for those big feelings. Be loving in your *no*. Stay with them. Hear them. As always, examine whether you can say *yes*, and say it as often as possible.

Sometimes, I catch myself saying no because—gulp—I have the parental power to say no, and I don't even know why I've said it. When I think about it objectively, though, I realize how much more often I can say yes. *Yes* gets easier the more we practice it. Plus, it feels much better to the nervous system!

CHAPTER 9:

FINDING CALM AS A PARENT

Here's the toughest part for many parents: oftentimes, when our child has seemingly gone off the rails, we feel dysregulated, too. And it's nearly impossible to create emotional or behavioral regulation in another human from *our* state of dysregulation.

Being angry, we may feel tempted to enforce an immediate punitive consequence if our child has committed an offense that bothers us, especially if this wasn't the first instance.

Although I don't recommend time-outs for children, I absolutely do recommend them for adults when they're having trouble controlling their anger. If an adult can create their own version of a calm-down corner and retreat to it for a moment while they collect themselves, that can be a very wise approach.

What does an adult's calm-down corner look like? For me, it's a comfy chair in the sunshine, often with a good book and a cup of tea. Other times, my calm-down corner is two minutes alone in the bathroom before my child finds me in there.

There are two caveats to adult time-outs:

1. Ensure the child is in a safe place while you take those moments to regroup.
2. Tell the child clearly that you're coming back and when they should expect you. Once again, if the child is too young to clearly understand how time works, try something like "I'll be calming down in the bathroom for the amount of time it takes you to watch one cartoon. Then I'll come back." The part about coming back is particularly important so the child doesn't feel abandoned.

Staying Cool in the Heat of the Moment

One important distinction we need to make when we're feeling triggered is to be aware of the difference between being triggered by our child, versus being triggered by our child's *behavior*.

It's easy, of course, to blame the child when we're upset. After all, the child is the one doing the thing that's upsetting us!

However, that's a trap with no good outcome. If we blame the child completely, that's fertile ground for anger and further power struggles.

When we're not consciously focused on peaceful discipline, our reaction might be to yell, accuse, shame, punish, or somehow use our internal angst to deal with the issue right in that moment. After all, why would our child act out or misbehave—seemingly intentionally—unless they've entirely lost their marbles? It's easy to get flustered and have a big, emotional reaction when things like this happen. Depending on our own attachment history (how we were or were not supported by our family of origin), we can unwittingly launch into fight, flight, freeze, or fawn mode:

- Fight: facing any perceived threat aggressively.
- Flight: running away from the danger.
- Freeze: unable to move or act against a threat.
- Fawn: immediately acting to try to please to avoid any conflict.[35]

For example, when we were growing up, if our primary caregiver did not make it safe for us to express our emotions, we may not feel safe in the presence of our child's emotions, either. If our parents fought back or yelled, we might be inclined to do these things with our own children. Alternatively, we might shrink or shrivel away from problems, sweeping them under the proverbi-

---

35 Mia Belle Frothingham, "Fight, Flight, Freeze, or Fawn: What This Response Means," Simply Psychology, October 6, 2021, https://www.simplypsychology.org/fight-flight-freeze-fawn.html.

al rug, or do whatever it takes to make things calm again. These can be normal responses to the wiring we learned when we were little (and yes, with practice, we can change our responses).

However, when it comes to conflict, we must remember that it's not parent versus child; it's parent and child versus whatever problem they're trying to solve. No one's winning; we're working together. We're on the same team.

CHAPTER 10:

PAUSING FOR THE HUG PROCESS

There is incredible power in the pause between input (in this case, our child's behavior) and reaction (in this case, ours). The part of our brains that evolved to respond quickly to stress is called the *amygdala*. In normal, non-chronic stress situations, it's quite small and helps us do things like move out of the way when our toddler hurls a toy truck at our head. It helps keep us safe instinctively.

However, because the amygdala is designed to keep us safe, it also has the incredible superpower of cutting off our rational thought to protect us. Author and traumatic stress expert Bessel van der Kolk, MD, calls it our "internal smoke detector."[36] It helps us instinctively sense danger even when we're not consciously looking for it. (This is also called *neuroception*.) However, the amygdala doesn't give us much time to think through whether our perceived threat is an actual threat.

When a stimulus happens (the toy truck hurtling toward our head), we react. This is good. However, we have about six seconds before the stress reaches our prefrontal cortex, where we can differentiate between "My toddler accidentally lost control of the truck while he was playing" and "My toddler is trying to harm me." If we get stuck in amygdala-land, we flip out. We lose it with our kid and may run away or fight back. It may translate to yelling as a perfectly normal biological response to getting a threat away from us. According to the *Harvard Business Review*:

---

36 Sam Himelstein, "Trauma and the Brain: An Introduction for Professionals Working with Teens," Center for Adolescent Studies, June 11, 2016, https://centerforadolescentstudies.com/trauma-and-brain/.

> When we perceive a threat, the amygdala sounds an alarm, releasing a cascade of chemicals in the body. Stress hormones like adrenaline and cortisol flood our system, immediately preparing us for fight or flight. When this deeply instinctive function takes over, we call it what Daniel Goleman coined in *Emotional Intelligence*, an "amygdala hijack." In common psychological parlance we say, "We've been triggered."[37]

When we want to parent peacefully, though, we need a way to stop this flood of stress hormones. In other words, we need to tell our brain that this is our child in front of us and not a charging mastodon.

Having six seconds to change our course of action before the amygdala takes over certainly isn't long. However, we can work with it. It's just about long enough to keep calm instead of turning into Parentzilla.

How do we do this?

The HUG Process

The HUG process helps us move from a place of emotional chaos to one of peace with our children. One key tenet of peaceful discipline is to know exactly this:

When challenges arise, it's us-with-our-child *against* the problem we're trying to solve.

The problem is external to our relationship. If we're able to see our child as innately trying to do the right thing (or acting out because their behavior is mirroring what they feel internally), we're less likely to blame and more likely to problem-solve alongside the child.

This is a critical shift in our thinking because it moves us away from authoritarian parenting and toward a more peaceful

37 Diane Musho Hamilton, "Calming Your Brain During Conflict," Harvard Business Review, December 22, 2015, https://hbr.org/2015/12/calming-your-brain-during-conflict.

and collaborative approach—that is, loving and healthy parental leadership that also respects the child.

With that as the preface, the HUG method is one way to keep calm(er) when you're upset. The three steps of the HUG method are:

- Hold your reaction
- Understand your child's perspective (get curious about your child's internal life rather than mad about their outward behavior)
- Give them grace to be human

H—Hold your reaction

For some people, taking a short inhale through the nose and doing a long, six-second exhale through the mouth can instantly thwart our stress response and help us pause. Why six seconds? Because it's a mechanism to remember how long we have to get a grip.

Pause and ask yourself, *How do I want to respond to my child in this moment? How do I want them to see me respond? What do I want them to remember about me as a parent?*

If the first idea that pops up stems from anger, ask, *Is it really what I want? Is my long-term desire coming from a place that promotes peace or conflict?*

Some parents find it helpful to imagine what their child is literally seeing in us, as if we're holding up a mirror and seeing exactly what they see. Is the child looking up at an overpowering and domineering adult whom they'd perceive as scary or even foolish, or is the child seeing a parent who's using healthy tools to manage their anger?

The anger itself doesn't have to go away. Anger, as one of the cornerstone emotions we feel, has beneficial and protective effects; it's our natural alert system. It's there to tell us when something isn't working for us. It's the *expression* of that anger that we need to monitor.[38]

38 Paul M. Litvak, Jennifer S. Lerner, Larissa Z. Tiedens, and Katherine Shonk, "Fuel in the Fire: How Anger Impacts Judgment and Decision-Making," *Portrait of the Angry Decision Maker: How Appraisal Tendencies Shape Anger's Influence on Cognition*" (2006).

This can be a great time to opt for a calm-down corner, time-in, or parenting time-out, as covered earlier.

If you take a parenting time-out, be careful not to stew on the problem and increase your anger. Instead, stretch, pray, meditate, draw, exercise,[39] or phone a friend. Do whatever grounds you.

If your body isn't looking for grounding but instead needs a release, you can trick your body by doing something unexpected. Jump. Dance. Wiggle your shoulders. Run five laps around your kitchen. Movement is healing.

Here's another scientifically backed approach you can try: smile.

What? Why would you want to smile when you're upset?

In short, when you move your facial muscles into a position that signifies happiness, these muscles send a message to your brain that you *are* happy. In fact, this approach can almost instantly lower your heart rate and blood pressure.

And it really is okay to pause to do these things. The trick is that you're not holding all reactions; you're holding your typical reaction (if it's the one you want to avoid). You're using this pause to teach your brain new and healthier patterns.

If you're worried that your child isn't learning from an immediate consequence of their actions, remember that the most important message they might learn in this moment is emotional regulation.

What about those times when you simply *can't* hold your anger or frustration entirely and channel it in a peaceful way?

I get it. You're not a robot, and I don't want you to be one. That doesn't model emotional authenticity. It models stuffing down emotions, and, as we've covered, that's dangerous territory. If this is your approach, the kettle will inevitably boil over sometimes.

There's an alternative, a middle ground you can use. If, for example, you're a yeller and you don't want to be one, you can

39 Strategies for Controlling Your Anger: Keeping Anger in Check," American Psychological Association, 2011, https://www.apa.org/topics/anger/strategies-controlling.

work on not being one. In this moment, though, if it's all your nervous system will let you do, work with it rather than against it.

An Example:

One evening, I made dinner later than usual, and I was feeling stressed about getting my child to bed on time. Although I know it works best to physically move my body and walk over to her to say, "Let's go to the table now," my anxiety kept my feet planted on the ground in the kitchen, one room away from where she was.

I called out, "Please come to dinner! It's on the table, and it's getting late." No one came. I tried louder. "Dinner's getting cold, and I really want to get you to bed on time!" Still no one.

What felt like fifty-two requests later (it was probably closer to three, each one increasing exponentially in stress), my frustration was clearly coming through in my voice. What child would want to come into a room with an audibly fuming parent?

At this point, I had the presence of mind to realize I was getting hyper-anxious and sounding awful to my child.

I knew I didn't want to be yelling. I knew my blood pressure was telling me to chill out. A little voice in the back of my head told me I was going about it all wrong.

Then, suddenly, I realized I did not want to betray my nervous system and pretend to feel peaceful. I just plain felt like yelling.

So, I tried a new approach. I let myself yell. In fact, I yelled with much more conviction.

I heard myself bellow, "Please get in here! Dinner is late and I'm super stressed and I'm worried we're going to have that penguin problem again!"

The next thing I knew, I had an eight-year-old at my side with a twinkle in her eye, asking, "What penguin problem?"

I responded, "You know how I hate it when we have dinner late. Remember that one time we ate too late and we turned into penguins? Oh, that was awful!"

Giggling, she moved to the sink and started washing her

"flippers" so we could eat the "sardines" I'd put on the table. Dinner was lovely and peaceful from that point forward.

I'll share more on this approach and why it works later, but the key takeaway here is that when you can't find your calm, you can channel your big feelings into something useful. The element of surprise can really change the energy in a room.

Children are watching how you use all your calming tools, along with whatever else you need to do to change the trajectory of the experience. With practice, they'll grow to model them.

While you're holding your reaction or redirecting it in a way that feels emotionally safe to you and your child (as some say, *practicing the pause*), your heart rate should regulate and you can move onto the *U* of the HUG process.

By the way, one word of caution: if you feel like hitting something, even a pillow, try a big self-hug instead. According to Dr. Ross Greene, we want to avoid pairing anger with physical aggression lest we train our brains to act out physically. Hugging yourself tightly is still physical, but it sends your body calming messages.

U—Understand your child's perspective

Ask yourself this: *From their perspective, what might have driven their behavior?*

If you find yourself mentally launching into accusations, return to the *H*—Hold your reaction. Dig deeper.

Put yourself in your child's shoes. Did something happen that made them feel disconnected? Were they seeking attention, which you can reframe as seeking connection? What's going on in their world that might've been the impetus for their action? They might not have the words to articulate what it was, but it's always somewhere beneath the surface.

As unlikely as it may feel in the moment, children *want* to do well for us. Try to give them the same benefit of the doubt that we'd want if we'd somehow behaved suboptimally. We'd want others to understand what motivated us to do it, deep inside. This is hard but important work.

Contrary to popular (albeit outdated) opinion, children aren't manipulative little misers who are always trying to get their way. They're doing the best they can to simply get their needs met, just like we all are. Plus, what if the basic need they're trying to get is something as straightforward as affection?

Once you've worked to understand your child's perspective, the natural human response is often compassion. It doesn't necessarily mean you agree with them; it means you value their humanity.

Look at the big picture from the framework of peaceful discipline. Have they experienced changes in their life that are causing stress in ways you might not have realized were related? Are they feeling connected to you, their siblings, and their classmates? Are they working to learn a new skill that's feeling hard for them? Are they grieving or reliving an old wound or suffering some other disappointment? Or, more simply, did they get enough sleep last night? Are they hungry or thirsty? Are they going through a growth or developmental spurt? Perhaps fighting an illness that hasn't surfaced yet?

You can empathize with whatever they've been processing and start thinking more objectively about what's motivated their behavior. Once you've let yourself drift into empathy, move on to the *G* of the HUG process.

An Example:

One day when my daughter was seven, she was in an unusually foul mood. She was giving me lots of back talk and was acting mad at life. For a while, I was dealing with it alright because my emotional cup was pretty full, but after an hour of it, I started to lose patience.

My unhappy tone started coming out with her. That certainly didn't make anything better. Hearing it in myself, though,

I realized I was contributing to the problem. I went through my mental checklist: Did she get enough sleep the night before? I thought so. Was she hungry? Nope, she'd just finished lunch.

And then I realized she'd barely had anything to drink that day. She'd refused her almond milk on her cereal that morning, didn't sip much of her water at lunch, and hadn't had anything in between.

Knowing that I've never met a child who says, "Yes!" to a glass of water when they're seemingly saying, "No!" to everything else in the world, I decided not to ask her. I just went to the fridge, grabbed her water with her favorite straw, and casually handed it to her. She gulped it down. Within about two minutes, she was completely back to normal—happy, playful, and as kind as can be.

No punishment or consequence would have addressed her behavior. What the kid needed was a glass of water.

G—Give them grace to be human

Oftentimes, if we can find the presence of mind to see their perspective, peaceful discipline will come about naturally from the compassion we've allowed to rise in our bodies.

As Dr. Ross Greene so aptly puts it, "Kids do well if they can." Resultantly, our job is to ask, "Why can't my child do well right now? What's going on?"

"I wonder . . ." statements work well here. So does "I'm curious about . . ." Invite your child to share their heart with you about what happened. If your child isn't volunteering an explanation (which is very, very common), it's fine for you to offer a theory. It might sound something like:

- "I wonder if you were feeling angry that I was on the phone for so long. Are you craving some special time together?"
- "I wonder if you're still feeling disconnected after our conflict this morning."

- "I wonder if you're worried about your upcoming school day."

In peaceful parenting, listen without defending; truly listen. Behind their actions, what is their *heart* trying to tell you?

Regardless of what they say, the message you want to drive home this moment is "You're safe to share your feelings with me without judgment or criticism."

Take whatever they offer as feedback to ponder. This can be your guidepost to figure out what they need. Odds are good that once that underlying need is met, they won't feel compelled to express it in the same way they did before.

An Example (this one comes from my husband's memory vault):

Once, when my husband was preschool age, he'd been corrected for doing something wrong (what it was, exactly, remains a mystery). He didn't like how the correction felt, so he decided to leave.

He packed his tiny toy suitcase with two essential items: clean underwear and a bunch of green grapes.

His parents watched him leave the house and walk two houses away to the end of the block (keeping him within sight the whole time). From their perspective, he could've been doing something else wrong. He was little and leaving the house without permission.

As it turns out, he had grand plans to walk, right then and there, 1,200 miles away to Disneyland. However, when he got to the aforementioned corner, toting his toy suitcase full of grapes and underwear behind him, he remembered that he wasn't allowed to cross the street. So, there he remained until he decided it was time to head home.

Now, from an adult perspective, it might've been tempting to chastise him further for breaking another rule—leaving—above and beyond whatever transgression he'd committed

in the first place. Alternatively, his parents could've held their reactions, which is what they did. They paused, observed, and got curious.

I don't know whether they dug deep enough to find out that it was emotional distress that had motivated him to leave, or what grace they gave him for doing so. I do know this, though—their having held on within the remits of safety, rather than racing after him, was enough for him to process his choices and make a better plan. There's a lot of empowerment to both parent and child when we simply "hold on" before we react.

Children often course-correct when we give them the space and the grace to do so.

It may be helpful to keep the following reminder handy (I've sometimes been tempted to get it as a tattoo):

THE "HUG" PROCESS
FOR STAYING PEACEFUL

H — **HOLD YOUR REACTION**
PAUSE and ground yourself. Ask "How do I WANT my child to see me responding?"

U — **UNDERSTAND THEIR PERSPECTIVE**
Ask "What does my child need right now? What kind of support are they seeking? If I assume the BEST of their intentions, what are those?"

G — **GIVE THEM GRACE TO BE HUMAN**
Just like all of us, kids are doing the best they can with the physical and emotional resources they have at the moment. Development isn't linear and their brains are still growing every day.

Won't Kids Learn They Can Get Away with Their Behavior?

Many of us were taught to believe that not addressing a child's behavior right away will teach them that they've gotten away with it.

This is not entirely true.[40]

Of course, the younger the child and/or the shorter their attention span, the more we want to keep teaching close to the incident in question. Still, even toddlers will learn best after co-regulation.

When kids are little, they literally can't retain information the way adults do, especially when they're feeling emotionally flooded. Their brains are too busy growing. At the same time, there are some important considerations to keep in mind.

For a young child, everything is a learning process, and they're largely driven by impulses. Their suboptimal behavior, when present, is not driven by malicious intent. If they push a plant off a plant stand, they were almost certainly curious about the plant or the stand, but their brain had not yet developed enough to think about the consequences of knocking it over or that the vase had once belonged to your grandmother. As such, it's important to reframe "intentionally being bad" as "naturally being curious." Early childhood never requires punishment.

The very young child truly is remembering a whole lot in any given moment. If a toddler has recently learned to walk and talk, they're still working on coordinating those things—and that requires an incredible amount of subconscious neurological processing. They're creating the neural pathways that help them remember how to do those things more and more easily with practice. With a brain already being that busy, it's natural that they'd forget to "always keep silverware on the table," for example.

---

40 Kristen Race, "Do Kids Benefit from Immediate Consequences," *The Mindful Life Blog* (2022).

For an older child—usually anything past toddlerhood—most teaching can be delayed a bit. You have a decent amount of latitude when it comes to how soon you need to revisit the situation before they forget about it. What's most important is to work on fostering a true, deep connection and ongoing secure attachment for the child.

Does the young child see that you're an emotionally safe place to turn to when they're upset, even if the upset is something they caused? That's what they need to know foremost for secure attachment.

On the flipside, it's dangerous for us to be both the source of their fear and their comfort. If the fear is great enough, it can lead to the opposite of secure attachment, which is disorganized attachment. A young child believes that if something bad happens to them, it's because *they* are bad. It's simply how their body processes it, and that can lead to ongoing and lifelong pain if left unresolved. They're unable to separate their "behavior" from their beliefs about themselves. Once again, if you want to learn more about attachment types, I recommend the work of Tina Payne Bryson, PhD, and Daniel J. Siegel, MD (specifically, *The Power of Showing Up*).

How that translates is that we can back off on immediate consequences for their actions and, instead, connect with them first. The most important lesson you can model for them in this moment is how to be aware of their own feelings, remain calm, and make connection-based decisions.

Be Proactive: Set Yourself Up to Succeed

Part of parents' ability to hold their reactions and use the HUG method when they're upset is having the emotional reserves to manage stressful situations when they arise.

Self-care feeds us those reserves. Self-care isn't optional; our kids need us to do it. If we won't do it for our own sake, maybe we're willing to do it so we can model for them how to slow down sometimes. By showing them that we matter to ourselves, we model that they should matter to themselves, as well.

But isn't self-care a cliché or, at best, some sort of magical unicorn?

It seems that in recent years, *self-care* has become a cliché—or worse, a dirty word. It can truly feel elusive for the exhausted parent.

Perhaps part of the problem is that society has managed to frame self-care as trips to the spa, a child-free night out, an impromptu exotic vacation—which very few of us find even remotely feasible most of the time. At least occasionally, many of us fall into bed, exhausted, thinking of all the things we didn't accomplish that day.

Reframing self-care can be immensely helpful. It can take many forms. These are just a few that I do personally. Perhaps some of them resonate with you, or perhaps your list looks very different:

- Holding your cup of coffee or tea with both hands to feel the warmth radiate into your body
- Taking belly breaths for a few minutes upon waking or before falling asleep at night
- Canceling scheduled activities that feel draining rather than uplifting (I have some tendency toward introversion, but there are other times I really need to feel connected to others)
- Connecting spiritually
- Engaging in any form of bodily self-care
    - A warm bath you can reliably take one night a week
    - Comfortable clothes (don't underestimate the power of cozy socks and stretchy pants)
    - A few minutes in the sunshine
    - Healthy food choices (cooking is not required; grabbing an apple counts)

- Setting and lovingly enforcing healthy boundaries with not only your children but also with other family members and friends
- Spending time in nature
- Talking to or visiting a faraway friend, especially a lifelong friend who knows you inside and out, and who can remind you of who you really are no matter how much your circumstances may have changed
- Gifting yourself scheduled screen time (or screen-free time) rather than constantly "checking in"

What brings you joy and comfort?

It's also important to note that many people wrongly believe that self-care must exclude other people. Some adults thrive on "me time" without anyone else around. Others get their "supercharging" from engaging in any form of levity or play with their friends, children, or partners. It all counts, and assuming your choices are healthy ones, there's no wrong way to recharge. You know yourself best.

The trick to every single form of self-care is to be able to count on it. Be intentional about it; don't just wait for it to happen. I've never spontaneously ended up in a bubble bath and wondered how I got there.

Certainly, if you see an opportunity to take care of yourself, seize it in the moment. However, we're likely to appreciate it even more if we make commitments to ourselves and keep them. We matter, too.

We get to put attending to our own needs on our to-do list—and prioritize them in realistic ways.

When we do this, it's truly amazing how much more patience we have for others (and ourselves, too) in moments of tricky parenting. In this sense, self-care truly is magical.

An Example:

After several years of chronic sleep deprivation, I finally started listening to my body and began to go to bed when I got tired at night. I didn't care if my child had only been asleep for thirty minutes and I was losing my whole evening. To the extent that I felt refreshed the next day—and treated everyone around me better, including myself—this was one of the best changes I've made. I learned I legitimately need a whole lot more sleep than I'd thought I did!

Somewhat to my surprise, my natural state isn't grumpiness, depression, or anxiety. When I'm rested, I rarely feel any of those things. I feel much more like the eternal optimist and "can-do-er" that I was before I decided my sleep didn't matter so much.

Once I spent a while catching up, I could go back to having some later nights to get things done or have fun, and I had much stronger reserves from which to draw.

CHAPTER 11:

DISTRACTING CHILDREN FROM TROUBLE: FRIEND OR FOE

Let's say that a young child wants to play with the scissors that are on the desk. We know that these scissors are sharp and not an age-appropriate toy. So, we trade the scissors for a stuffed animal, and the child initially seems all right with that trade.

After a few moments, though, the child wants the scissors back. We lovingly hold the limit, explain that the scissors are too sharp, and put them away in a safe place. Then, the child falls apart emotionally. There is nothing in the world that they want more than those pointy, shiny scissors. It's stabby thing or nothing for them.

Common approaches to handling the child's intense emotional response include the following:

- Distraction
- Telling the child they're okay
- Reminding the child that they can't have the scissors

Why don't each of these suffice?

- Distraction alone doesn't address the child's feelings. When we do this, we inadvertently, albeit with the best intentions, communicate to the child that we don't see what's important to them. Certainly, it's good to give the child a safe alternative (i.e., the stuffed animal), but many parents keep searching for the right distraction, meaning one that works. While the child might calm down and we, therefore, feel that it did work, the only thing we've really succeeded in doing is quieting the child if the scissors go unmentioned. We did not address their hurt or disappointment.

- Telling the child they're okay is dismissive. Many of us clearly remember being told by our parents, "You're okay, you're okay," when we were upset and clearly knew we weren't okay. The same would be true for us now, as adults, if another adult told us we were fine when we knew we weren't. We'd be annoyed as heck, wouldn't we?
- Reminding the child that they can't have the scissors simply perpetuates a power struggle. The child already knows they can't have the scissors because you've taken them away. They haven't forgotten, so there's no need to reiterate it. We don't need to be right when the scissors are already gone. No child is going to change their disappointment to acceptance simply by being told the same thing again.

What to try instead might go something like this:

First, acknowledge what's happening:

"I see how upset you are. You really wanted those scissors. I see how disappointed you're feeling. I'll help you through it. You're going to be okay." (The "going to be" differs from "you're okay" insofar as it gives the child hope without gaslighting them.)

Then, if they're still upset, state what you're going to do to co-regulate with them:

"I am going to sit right here with you and support you. All of your feelings are safe here." I specifically encourage "All of your feelings are safe here" because it is affirming for the child and it is a reminder to us, as the caregiver, that our job is to make sure our children's feelings really are safe here.

It's a reminder of our commitment to let our children have their feelings freely, without judgment or interruption.

Sure, we can keep that stuffed animal handy, but as a comfort item rather than as a distraction. Then, we proceed with that which is often incredibly challenging:

We wait. We might be silent, hum and/or rock the child, or gently repeat a calming phrase like "You're safe here." We simply stay present, touching our child lovingly and gently if that's soothing to them, and let them continue to express themselves as long as they need to.

At what point do we make it stop? When *do* we offer a distraction?

Here, it gets even trickier: we trust our child's timing above and beyond our own point of discomfort.

That is not to say that we dismiss our own feelings. It is, however, an invitation to ask ourselves in the moment, "Do I want my child to stop because I think it's best for my child, or is this about my own discomfort with their being so upset? Is their crying/yelling/expressing bothering them or me?"

Remember that crying is beneficial to the nervous system, provided that the child feels supported and nurtured in the process.[41] Leaving a child to cry alone is not beneficial unless the parent needs to temporarily leave the child for their safety (i.e., the parent feels too triggered by the crying and needs to step away to regulate their own emotions).

If the child is nearly done with their emotional release (which only the child would know), and the parent interrupts prematurely with a distraction, there will still be unfinished business for the child.

The child may perceive our interruption as "I was almost done crying, but then Mommy brought me these toys to play

41 Leo Newhouse, "Is Crying Good for You?," Harvard Health Publishing, Harvard Medical School, March 1, 2021, https://www.health.harvard.edu/blog/is-crying-good-for-you-2021030122020.

with, and I haven't fully processed what I was feeling. Now I have this cognitive dissonance of happy and upset, and I'm not sure what to do with that. She said all my feelings were safe here, but by doing this, I wonder if that's true." The child won't use these terms, of course, but it's essentially what happens in the brain, and it's understandably confusing.

Usually, when the child is emotionally supported, the child's turmoil will resolve on its own when the child is ready. Of course, the more pent-up sadness, anger, or frustration the child has, the longer or more frequently they might need to express themselves while they learn that it's safe to do so. If the child is tired, hungry, thirsty, or overwhelmed, you might prepare for some "bonus rounds" of big feelings until those core needs are addressed.

Just like the shortest distance between two points is a straight line, the shortest distance to the end of a big emotional release is to go straight through it.

Once the child is regulated again, it's often tempting to reiterate why we held the boundary in the first place. It's common to add a seemingly loving "I told you so" in the form of a lesson/wrap-up statement for the child. We might be inclined to say, "See? You were fine. That's why I didn't give the scissors back to you. I knew you'd be all right, and the scissors were too sharp." This, of course, would only open the emotional wound anew. Why sabotage ourselves?

Any form of parental dominance and control is unnecessary when we attempt to prove that we knew better than they did. Better is to simply let it go . . . for now. Move on to an activity that continues positive momentum and connection.

As soon as the child is relaxed and regulated again, it's the perfect time to delve into story teaching.

If, of course, the child quickly seems to pull back emotionally, give it a little while and try again. You know best when your child is likely to be receptive to hearing what you have to say.

CHAPTER 12:

GETTING THE CHILD "UN-STUCK" EMOTIONALLY

If the child seems to be ruminating (getting stuck repeatedly and looping on the same points for a long time), they might need help moving on to the next phase of their emotional expression.

How long is long? There's no set amount of time, unfortunately. Wouldn't it be nice if there were? Emotions resolve at their own pace. Trust your judgment and read your child's cues.

What kind of cues might the child be offering you?

Perhaps they're seeking regular eye contact and seemingly looking for guidance; perhaps they verbalize, "I don't know what to do," or "Make it stop!" Some children change their tone of voice, and the expression becomes more of a tired/bored sound. If they're tired or bored, they'll be more likely to loop emotionally—and nothing will "solve" the looping until they're rested or otherwise supported. Every child has their own way of asking for additional support.

They may also hit, push, or act out more physically. Recall in these moments that this behavior reflects their internal discomfort. Keep yourself and others safe, stay grounded as best you can, and gently but directly remind them that hitting hurts: "Hold your body still and I'll help you get through this." When you observe counterproductive behavior, it's all right to offer statements that might be helpful.

If holding space isn't enough and moving on isn't happening naturally, that's often a child's way to say they need a different approach.

Refrain from solving the child's problem for them, but you can certainly express your curiosity. "I wonder . . ." statements can prove especially useful here.

Examples:

- "I wonder if a hug would help."
- "I wonder if drawing a picture of your anger/sadness/frustration would help."
- "I wonder if some fresh air or a drink would help." (A simple change of scenery can work wonders!)

Many children are not receptive to being asked questions when they're upset, which is another reason I prefer the "I wonder . . ." statements. They can choose whether and how to respond.

You can also try these things without asking. You can lovingly direct: "Let's go outside" or "Here's your water." This approach can work well if the child is particularly upset and not willing or able to engage in dialogue with you.

Let your child process fully, and when they're ready, you can move on together. The "tantrum" will have fully resolved. There are no leftovers; there's no accumulated stress to save for the next big emotional release.

Now that the behavior has ceased, the emotional release has concluded, and connection has been restored, you can move on to story teaching!

Part 3:

HOW TO USE STORY TEACHING

CHAPTER 13:

UNDERSTANDING STORY TEACHING

Story teaching is a way to use storytelling to help the child process what's transpired (or what's going to transpire soon). It helps the child feel safe and emotionally supported while they learn.

Before I get into specific examples of story teaching, here are some general guidelines to consider:

Perhaps most importantly, don't overthink it! True, I've included lots of ideas here, and they can help. But you know your child best.

Timing: Story teaching can occur at one of three times.

- **Preventively:** before a scenario for which you're trying to prepare your child occurs
    - Examples: learning to use the toilet, preparing to move house or deal with another major life event, increasing a child's comfort level with an out-of-the-ordinary situation, such as going to a noisy birthday party
- **In the moment:** when something's not going as planned
    - Examples: seeing the child make a mess they're not supposed to be making, helping a child transition to an activity that's hard for them, dealing with a recurring trouble spot (such as bedtime or school drop-off)
- **Restoratively:** after a problematic or difficult event has transpired

- Examples: helping the child process an unexpected loss or disappointment, helping the child make sense of something confusing that's happened, such as a conflict with a friend or sibling (or even with you)

A word of caution: if your child has just had a particularly long or big emotional release, it may feel too raw to them to start learning through stories. Emotional exhaustion is real. If necessary, give it some time.

Logistically speaking, there's other timing to consider, too. What time of day is your child most receptive to stories and quiet time with you? I'm going to go out on a limb and guess that it's not while they're on top of a jungle gym or hungry right before dinner.

Is bedtime their peaceful place for stories? One ubiquitous truth of childhood is that kids love staying up past their bedtime. Perhaps start the bedtime routine ten minutes early so you can squeeze in a story with an important message you'd like to convey. The actual lights-out time doesn't need to change if you're concerned about that, but I'd bet that kids will feel extra special, and extra attentive, if they perceive this quality time—one-on-one story time with you—as a unique treat for them.

Also, there's something sacred about being in the dark together. Some children are more prone to processing their experiences aloud with you when they're in the peaceful safety of darkness together (dim lights often work just as well).

If not at bedtime, find another place in your family rhythm that's typically good for connection. We all have a natural ebb and flow to our days. When is your child usually open-minded, peaceful, and still? That's your green light!

Characters: The characters of your stories can vary. Try using:

- People your child actually knows in real life (including your child)
- Fictional characters you make up that may or may not resemble your child in behavior or temperament

- Pets or other animals, real or imaginary
- Recurring characters across one or more evolving storylines
- Onetime characters you introduce for a specific purpose

When you create a character to whom you'd like your child to relate, make sure to include some of your child's favorite things. Does your child love the color yellow? Describe the character as having yellow hair or a yellow backpack. Does your child love dinosaurs? You know what your main character has to be. Does your child love raspberries? Their mirror-character loves them, too. You get the idea. You want the character to resonate with them.

Further, you can use your judgment or ask your child whether the main character should share your child's name. A variation of their name is very personal yet helpful for making it feel emotionally safe. Adding a title can be especially effective.

Jeremy might enjoy being "Veterinarian Jeremy" and Kristen might enjoy being "Airplane Pilot Kristen," for example. What are your child's passions? Incorporate them in these titles as well. Royal titles can be fun, as can other made-up titles of prestige or perceived importance. Children, just like adults, enjoy feeling that they have influence.

The more relatable and naturally likeable your character is to your child, the more they'll see themselves in that character. You want them to connect emotionally and consider the character their ally. Through your story, this character is going to be their teacher and role model.

One word of caution: if the child's acting uncomfortable with the story or the character you've selected, the scenario may be feeling too close for comfort. It can help to redirect the story or ask the child if they'd prefer a name, character, or venue change.

When it comes to the temperament and behavior of the characters you choose, please choose characters and behaviors that aren't perfect. No one can live up to that ideal. What we want is for children to resonate and connect with the characters, and to learn that their whole selves are welcome in your family—tricky behavior and all!

In your stories, show compassion and understanding for the character who's struggling. Their character, literally and metaphorically, is never "bad." Who shows up to emotionally support them? To give them a hug? To care for them and love them even when they're at their worst? When you tell stories that reinforce the strength of your relationship (or where you want it to be); their courage or resilience; or any other message you're trying to convey, they can see themselves mirrored in the story. This can be really powerful.

Child's Age: Fortunately, there is no maximum age at which story teaching completely stops being effective. As a general guideline based on brain development,[42] however, this can help:

- Under seven: Tell clear stories; most children are still pretty literal at this age. Animal stories are often popular with this age group, and they translate pretty well to human interactions.
- Seven to twelve: Use literal and clear stories that may use more real and relatable characters, but with more elements of excitement and fantasy. Generally, by this age, children can make bigger leaps between concrete and abstract concepts.
- Twelve and older: Choose stories rooted in reality, often linked to real-life situations that have transpired. For older children, it's often useful to have the main characters be those outside the home so that it feels more emotionally safe and engaging to them (especially if the characters are, or were, in the child's peer group at the time of the main story event). It's fine to use

42 Kendra Cherry, "Piaget's Four Stages of Cognitive Development Explained," Verywell Mind, last modified, May 2, 2022, https://www.verywellmind.com/piagets-stages-of-cognitive-development-2795457.

yourself at your child's age if the child is interested in those stories. If not, choose another main character. By this age, stories tend to be much more concrete and transparent. These are often stories about real or fictional people the child knows from their own experiences. The key here is relatability.

With older children, you'll want to tailor your story to their motivating factors, as Kim John Payne describes in his helpful book *The Soul of Discipline*. According to his research and experience:

- Some children enjoy being problem-solvers and are often motivated by action
- Some are interested in the nuances of relationships and emotional expression
- Virtually all children want to succeed and master tasks

You know your child best, and certainly these concepts may apply to younger children, too. Try elements of each that vary and see what sticks.

Length of Story

The optimal length is dependent largely on the child's willingness to sit and listen comfortably without being "made" to stay in the story teacher's presence. Stories don't need to be complex; they need to be compelling and clearly understandable.

Some stories are only a couple of minutes long. Others can be ongoing with recurring characters facing new challenges.

Although this is a generalization, it's often safe to assume that very young children prefer shorter stories. Their attention span (or willingness to sit and listen to a parent speak) tends to be capped at just a few minutes.

The sweet spot for longer stories often begins in that magical time around age six or seven. There are exceptions, of course. Some kids are wigglier than others (which is not to say that story time has to be a stationary event)!

How Many Stories You'll Need—and Some Very Good News for You

Excellent news here: you don't need to be a walking encyclopedia of entertaining stories. According to Dr. Ross Greene, most problematic behavior is predictable.[43] Knowing this, we can home in on a few repeat offenders (familiar problems) and create stories that address them.

That's a relief, isn't it? If your child has never stolen a thing, for example, you don't need to have a story on hand about stealing. No lying or hair pulling or social anxiety or sibling rivalry in your home? Great! You don't need stories about those topics, either.

What topics do appear to be on rinse and repeat in your home? Those are the problems for which you can create problem-solving stories. Most families have only a few recurring pain points (although new developmental stages can certainly come with new surprises).

And for bonus good news, once you've told a story that addresses whatever problem you're dealing with a couple of times (give or take a bunch of times, depending on the child), your child likely won't need the whole story ever again. Either that, or you'll become so good at telling it that you can do it on autopilot.

Often, however, you can remind your child in the moment, "Hey, remember how Billy Bovine handled the situation with Peter Parrot? Yeah—you can do that again here." That's enough to resurrect the point of the story in your child's memory—how the problem was solved and what you're gently asking of the child now. Plus, when you take this approach, at least two good things happen:

- You're not shaming or embarrassing your child for their behavior; you're talking about fictional characters as reminders. Much safer emotionally!

43 Dandelion Seeds, "Interviews with Parenting & Child Development Experts," Dandelion-Seeds.com (2022).

- Your child's executive function skills grow yet again; they're remembering something they learned in the past and applying it to diverse situations.

Trust me, it's so much easier at the playground to call out something from a story you've invented like, "Maven Raven!" and have your young child return a look of understanding than it is to march over and awkwardly intervene when you sense trouble brewing between friends. I mean, what kid wants their mom or dad to call them out in obvious ways? It's like you get a whole new set of magical code words. (Just be sure not to call out something that other kids might bestow upon your child as an unwelcome nickname. No teen needs friends who remind them of that one time their mom called them Fruity Patootie.)

Story Selection and Topics

Part of the reason I prefer homemade stories—the ones adults create specifically for the children in their care—is exactly because they're personal and customized. Not only can the adult choose the topic, they can also obtain real-time feedback from the child via the child's engagement, body language, and even their requests for plot twists to see what's working for them.

Conversely, pre-written stories from outside sources can be great starting points for parents to use. I've listed some authors I like in the resources section.

Of course, there are many others beyond these. Your local librarian, bookseller, or an Internet search can help you find them. There are many resources available online and in print for pre-written stories that address specific behaviors and other challenges. Gauge your child's level of sensitivity and awareness and modify the stories as necessary if you're the one reading them to the child. Still, in my experience, personalized stories work best.

CHAPTER 14:

SETTING THE BAR (LOW)

Fortunately for us, children are incredibly forgiving when it comes to the quality of stories. What they love is simply being with us, having our full attention, and feeling our active engagement. Plotlines don't need to be thoroughly thought out; character development can nearly go by the wayside—just like it does in many children's "easy reader" books.

An Example:

I'll never forget the time my five-year-old daughter walked up to me and said, "Mama, Daddy started a story for me but didn't have time to finish it. Can you tell me what happens in it?"

"Sure, baby. How did he start it?" I figured I'd improvise.

She replied with all the innocence that comes naturally to a five-year-old, "He said, 'Three men walked into a bar and went up to the bartender.' What happens next, Mama?"

Thanks for that, Daddy.

I continued with a benign and silly story about the men ordering lemonade and the bartender simply sticking straws into lemons, which she found incredibly funny. I added a teaching point about how being flexible in life is good and how it's helpful to know that we won't always get what we ask for in life. We can still find ways to make things work.

Children's stories about bars aside (ahem), feel free to use the premise of other stories as the basis for your own. Children won't mind if you retell a story you've read elsewhere (or previewed for them). You can give it an alternate ending; customize it to make it more appropriate for their age level, level of sensitivity, readiness, or specific situation. Modify the details of the characters to make them more relatable for your child.

Interestingly, and as challenging as it may sound, some of the best stories are the ones we simply start telling without having a full roadmap in our minds. Just get started with something. Use what you know of other stories, and let your words flow from there. All you need to decide ahead of time is the main point you want to get across. Let the characters you create find their own ways there as you speak.

Some great ways to start, as evidenced by how often they're employed, include these options:

- "Once upon a time, there was a girl/boy/unicorn/dog/dinosaur who . . ."
- "When I was your age, something like this happened to me! Would you like to hear about it?"

Stories—simple or complex, well planned or impromptu—are wonderfully connecting. Unless we're specifically going for a storytelling award, we can trust that if the listener is staying put and engaged, our stories are good enough exactly as they are. We can eliminate the pressure to tell a "great" story and, instead, just tell one that our child enjoys. That is enough.

What If I Just Can't Come Up with Stories?

I encourage you to not only rely on your own imagination but also to incorporate existing books that have a clear lesson that is readily apparent to both parent and child.

Likewise, it's equally important to enjoy some stories together where there's no agenda or moral that you're trying to instill.

Stories purely for the sake of entertainment are also immeasurably valuable.

If you have trouble coming up with stories, that's okay. Ask your child to co-tell one with you. Perhaps they come up with the character and setting, and you provide the plotline. Perhaps you modify a story you've heard elsewhere, even if you simply change the names of the characters.

The good news about story teaching is that the content can come from almost anywhere.

What If the Child Doesn't Like It?

Part of the beauty of story teaching is that you don't need to follow a script. For example, you might start with "Once upon a time, a chipmunk sat next to a tree, wondering if she'd ever be big enough to scamper all the way up to its tippy-top branches."

If your child cuts you off and demands that the chipmunk start to fly, guess what? You've just created the world's first flying chipmunk. Go with it. It's all good. In fact, letting your child help tell the story can be a wonderfully effective way to engage them and hold their interest.

For an older child, you might hear this: "[Groan.] Not another story about when *you* were little." Okay—that's your cue to respond with something specific that's likely to hold their attention. They're giving you a gift by essentially saying, "That approach won't teach me anything, but maybe I'll listen to something else." If need be, jump straight to the climax: "What if I told you it was one of the scariest things I've ever done?" *That's* intriguing.

Try using a funny accent. Stand up if you've been sitting; sit down if you've been standing. Have fun. Be as theatrical as you're comfortable being (unless the sheer embarrassment of your child tells you to keep your inner Broadway star behind your shower curtain). Animation generally begs attention.

Not comfortable being "onstage" in front of your kids? That's okay, too. Be you. Be relatable and real. Kids often find comfort in the familiar. We all do.

What If Your Child Sabotages Your Plan for the Story?

Eighteenth-century poet Robert Burns wrote, "The best laid plans of mice and men often go awry." He wasn't wrong.

We can have the perfect story lined up to instill the message we want our child to take away from our brilliant storytelling prowess, and suddenly, our child throws us a curve ball. This can happen for a lot of reasons, including:

- The point you're making is too heavy-handed or moralistic (in other words, you're overdoing it)
- It hits too close to home emotionally and they're uncomfortable
- They're feeling playful and goofy and just want to take the story elsewhere for the fun of it
- They love your story and don't ever want it to end (I also call this "every night at bedtime")

It's all right if this happens for any of these reasons or others. All it really means is that the child wasn't ready for the story you planned to tell. No matter how great it was, they weren't in the optimal place to internalize your message.

Rather than fight against it and *make* your story happen as you planned (which is sure to only exacerbate the situation and frustrate you if your efforts are thwarted again), just go with it. Turn it into a fun, or ridiculous, or whatever-it-needs-to-be story instead. Celebrate your child's creativity. Honor their explicit or implicit boundaries. Follow their lead.

You can always come back later to the point you were attempting to make and try again. Perhaps your child will be more receptive to it by then, or perhaps there's another way to approach the topic.

And if the "problem" is that they never want the story to end, consider that a gift. You can find good pausing points, rather like chapters of a book, and continue as appropriate. Personally, I create some limits around when I'll tell stories, such as at bedtime or every morning after we brush teeth. Otherwise, I'd be a nonstop storytelling machine. Mama needs a breather sometimes.

CHAPTER 15:

FOLLOWING THE STEPS

Many of us likely remember from writing class that stories have the following components:

- Exposition (introduction)
- Rising action
- Climax
- Falling action
- Resolution

While story teaching contains those components, this is not intended to be a quiz on how well you remember each of the steps. More important is to remember the gist of what you want to communicate—what you want to teach.

In much simpler terms, story teaching includes:

- Introduction (usually only one or two characters, setting, peaceful vibe)
- Problem concept
- Emotion coaching (part 1)
- Resolution
- Emotion coaching (part 2)

Easier to remember, yes?

Here's a look at each section in a bit more detail.

Introduction

The introduction in story teaching is designed to engage the child's interest. We want the story to feel emotionally safe and peaceful. Use it to build connection and a sense of trust.

What not to do: "Once upon a time, there was a boy named [your child's name] who wouldn't listen to his grandfather at bedtime."

What to try instead: "Once upon a time, there was a squirrel whose ears fell off every night at bedtime." (Note: I'll share my version of this story in the sample stories. Also, if your listener is very young and/or very literal, you might want to reassure them that ears rarely fall off of their own accord.)

The most effective teaching stories have only one or perhaps two characters, unless the story is specifically designed to address problems with groups. Simple is best. Not only is it easier for the storyteller, it's also easier for the child to follow. Most of us are not professional storytellers, so the more easily we can stick to the point, the better.

As for the setting, find something that's unique and entertaining for the child. If, for example, the story takes place outdoors, why not make it outdoors on another planet? Rather than a story about two children who can't seem to get along, why not make it two snowy owls? Have fun with it.

Be as creative as you can while still staying true to simplicity. Of course, like most things, the more you practice, the more easily creativity will come to you.

If creativity isn't your forte, it's perfectly fine to put two normal children in a normal, everyday backyard—real, familiar concepts can also be very anchoring in a story. All good!

Problem Concept

This is where you introduce the behavior, or a reasonable likeness thereof, that you want to address with your child.

Why not just introduce it directly without a story? Of

course, that's a viable option if your child is open to it and it feels peaceful to both of you (your approach has much to do with how the child will internalize it). If there's any tension around the topic, however, stories are a great way to address the issue with less risk of shaming or blaming the child, while still getting the point across.

Trust your instincts and your child's cues about how close to home you want it to feel. For example, let's say that your child has a lot of trouble with transitioning from one activity to another.

What not to do: "Jimmy wouldn't leave the couch when it was time for school, and it really made his mama mad."

What to try instead: "After Jimmy ate the superglue, he realized that he couldn't move! Oh no—he was totally stuck right where he was—and the bus was already coming up their block!" (Of course, if the child is very young, make it clear that glue is not edible. Maybe he gets stuck in a giant roll of tape instead.)

Emotion Coaching (Part 1)

Emotion coaching has two key components:

- Identifying/naming the feeling(s)
- Understanding why those feelings are present

In story teaching, it's important to help the child uncover (perhaps with your help) what they imagine the character facing the problem might be feeling. If the child can discern the character's feelings on their own, it may give you some insight into their motivation for behaving the way they did. Alternatively, if they don't perceive the story to be about them, it's still helpful for them to verbalize what they suspect is motivating the character.

Young children will need a lot of practice naming emotions, especially those that may feel unsafe, scary, or overwhelming to them. It's important to recall that adults have much more experience managing anger, for example, whereas it might feel "too big" for a child to navigate confidently, in stories or otherwise.

Story teaching can mitigate and normalize some of the big feelings kids have about, well, their own big feelings.

As such, after you present the problem concept, pause to investigate what the character might be feeling. It helps build your child's emotional literacy if you ask simply and directly, "Wow, what do you think they're feeling right now?"

Depending on the child's age and emotional maturity, it might behoove you to explain why the character feels that way (or engage your child in describing it). This is a great way to connect the dots for kids who are still practicing this skill.

For younger children and/or those who are early in the process of growing their emotional literacy, it's best to focus the emotion coaching on a single feeling (angry, scared, etc.). That's easiest to comprehend and digest.

For older children and/or those who have a greater comfort level with the complexity of emotions, touch on as many feelings as you're comfortable addressing in a single story. It can be very helpful for children to know that it's normal to feel two or more emotions at once.

For example, a child might feel conflicted about needing to go to school, as in "I'm sad I have to go to school today, but I'm happy to see my friends again." Normalizing having mixed feelings can help the child feel more peaceful about multilayered topics.

Naturally, the more feelings you introduce because of your problem concept, the more you'll need to remember to fully resolve at the end of your story. Keep it simple for yourself, and for your listener, whenever possible.

Further, recall that at this point in emotion coaching, the emotions that feel harder than others to children are likely to be the ones at the forefront of your problem concept. This will happen quite naturally in your story teaching.

Resolution

Depending on the age and emotional readiness of the child, this is where children's aha moments often happen—and the teaching is particularly effective.

If your child is young or not yet ready for this part of the exercise, you can model through the story what the character should do about the problem concept. It's important to empower the child in this section. Resolution must come from within rather than from some external force that saves the day. We want our child to be the hero, to internalize and recognize their success.

Even if another character guides or suggests the resolution, the onus is on the character with the problem to embrace it and own their part. You can also encourage them to discuss what not to do and why.

What not to do: "Jaden's daddy sprayed the Nightmare Dragon with dragon spray, and the Nightmare Dragon never visited Jaden again."

What to try instead: "Jaden's daddy showed Jaden how to hold the bottle of dragon spray and explained how to use it. The next time the Nightmare Dragon showed up, Jaden bravely sprayed it, and much to his surprise, the dragon turned into a sweet little bunny rabbit."

Along with the child being the owner of the solution, include the *why*. For some children, the reason for the resolution won't be obvious. To continue the example, it would be important to add something to the effect of "Jaden could've asked his daddy to spray the dragon, but Jaden knew he had to find the magic of his inner strength for it to work best."

If the child is feeling too anxious about addressing the issue on their own, perhaps your initial version of the story has the parent and child facing the problem together first, before the child tackles it solo.

Emotion Coaching (Part 2)

If you've done your part up until now, the child might well be seeking full resolution not only of the problem concept but also of whatever internal strife transpired during the story. It's not done yet.

We crystallize the teaching best when we help the child *feel* the character's new way of behaving. How does this work?

It's brain science—specifically, mirror neurons. Here's how they work:

> Mirror neurons are a class of neuron that modulate their activity both when an individual executes a specific motor act and when they observe the same or similar act performed by another individual.[44]

I describe these feelings, beliefs, and experiences as being contagious. Does this mean that if I get the hiccups you'll get them, too? No, but there's some chance that even by my mentioning the word *hiccups*, your breath changed a little. Without any conscious effort on our part, our bodies react on some level as if the things that are happening to others are also happening to us.

We can also observe others' emotions, and that's why we use emotion coaching not once but twice in stories. This observation can work effectively in the mind's eye, which is exactly what story teaching provides. Plainly put, if the child can imagine an event along with a feeling, the brain will respond to some degree as if the event and feeling actually happened. They can "feel" the resolution and feel the emotion that we want them to associate with the situation being handled.

That said, this is not a form of control-based parenting. We can't and shouldn't try to "make" anyone else feel what we want them to feel, despite the influence of mirror neurons. Stories are an invitation, and we should very much account for our child's

44 J. M. Kilner and R. N. Lemon, "What We Know Currently about Mirror Neurons," *Current Biology* (December 2013).

unique and authentic experiences and preferences.

Who knew brain science could be part of story teaching?

Just like in the first instance of emotion coaching within a story, it's often helpful for the child to fully engage in how it feels for the character to have resolved the problem—rather than to just be told how a character is feeling. This way, it's like they've watched it on a movie screen and "felt" along with the main character.

Remember, the two key components that must be present are:

- Identifying/naming the feeling(s)
- Understanding why those feelings are present

Bring your child to full comprehension by helping them describe what they imagine the character feels and why.

The *why* often requires some adult guidance, and it's a good reminder for us, too, to avoid rushing the emotional resolution.

What not to do: "Aya broke her brother's toy but felt really happy when she fixed it."

What to try instead: "Aya had accidentally broken her brother's toy and felt sad about it. When she figured out how to fix it, she released her sad feelings and realized that, instead, she felt relieved and peaceful. She knew that her brother would be happy with the toy again, and she felt proud of herself for having figured out how to repair it."

Executive Functioning Bonus Points

For a child who's older and/or more emotionally aware, it can be highly beneficial to stop telling the story at certain points—usually before the sections on emotion coaching—to ask the child what they think the characters are feeling.

The more practice they get imagining others' perspectives in story teaching, the more they train their brains to consider others' perspectives in real life.

As I touched on earlier, you can pause and ask questions like, "What do you think the character should do?" Talking through options without judgment can be insightful—not only to help you understand your child's current state of mind but also to help them flex their decision-making muscles.

If the child suggests an alternative that doesn't model good judgment (for example, the child suggests hitting when the character feels upset), rather than condemning the child's contribution to the story, validate the feeling behind the desire to follow through on the undesirable behavior.

In this example, you might say, "Mmmm. I can see how being that mad might make someone want to hit. They're so, so mad!" If the child is really needing to sit with the feeling of anger (or whatever big feeling they're experiencing), don't rush the peaceful resolution. It's much more important that they feel their feelings and come to emotional resolution than be pushed along to sunshine and rainbows. We want emotional authenticity. No child will crave peaceful resolution if they're still boiling inside.

Of course, once the big feelings do pass and they're ready to listen and/or participate, you can help them consider more peaceful options instead.

Whenever it's time to transition, rather than telling them their suggestion is wrong, stick with the validation of the feelings behind the action. From there, you can add, "Hitting hurts, so I wonder what a peaceful option would be that still helps them handle their anger."

Help the child come up with peaceful and positive solutions seemingly on their own, and they'll be more likely to retain that message when that situation, or a reasonable facsimile thereof, presents itself in real life.

These are, indeed, executive-functioning skills in action.

CHAPTER 16: NURTURING HAPPY ENDINGS

You may notice that in all the examples I share, each one has a happy ending.

You may wonder, what's the point? Don't some stories not turn out so well, and aren't the original fairy tales infamous for unhappy endings? I mean, in the earliest versions, the heartbroken girl in *Little Mermaid* turns into sea foam, the *Frog Prince* gets thrown at a wall before achieving marital bliss, and the character upon which *Sleeping Beauty* is based wakes up surprised to learn she already has twins. These are disturbing stories that I'd hardly call "happily ever after."

Sure, in real life (and in many fairy tales), tricky situations don't always end with making up, feeling good, and being strong.

What we're attempting to do here, however, is to create a growth mindset in the way kids approach life. We're teaching them to have a glass-half-full mentality.

Modeling how tricky situations can turn out well helps encourage kids to find solutions to their problems—and helps them to realize they can do this consistently, even in the face of adversity.

We want to nourish their executive-functioning skills by actively engaging them in problem-solving. Problem-solving doesn't happen as fully or as naturally when we show them how their solutions won't work.

By the same token, if your child is struggling with disappointment or perfectionism, then definitely create a story in which the protagonist learns to accept their mistakes (and their full, authentic, flaw-normalized self)! Their solutions might not work out, but their self-compassion and self-acceptance will.

Throw some "what-not-to-do moments" and failed attempts into your stories. Resilience is a powerful teacher. It likely wouldn't be helpful for a child to see their protagonist experience nothing but success.

There is a place for unhappy endings, of course. There's both science and logic behind *Grimms' Fairy Tales* being so, well, grim. It is certainly an important message to help kids understand that life doesn't always turn out rosily. At the same time, however, we want to raise optimistic kids who feel empowered to go on when life hands them lemons.

If you choose to have an unhappy ending, make sure the child's emotional resolution of that ending is still one of hope.

One more point to consider: sometimes kids really do push for a grim ending and don't want things to turn out all right. If this is the case for your child, you can engage them in co-crafting a story just for the purpose of entertainment. As long as it's age appropriate, that's fine. Alternatively, they may legitimately be trying to see if they can handle hard topics. Especially if they've witnessed something stressful, they may need the space to simply be with those tricky feelings in the emotional safety of your presence. This can help build their resilience.

CHAPTER 17:

RETURNING TO THE *WHY*

Teaching children in ways that are both gentle and beneficial to their learning is a critical component of creating a more peaceful world. This work starts with us.

When we give our children the opportunity to think creatively about the situations they face in everyday life, it not only helps them deal with reality but also supports the investment they make in being authors of their own life stories.

When they can start to see different outcomes to situations they're facing, they learn to not only accept the parts they can't control, but also to be more active creators of their own destinies. They can manage the trickiness of life more gracefully, knowing that if their "story selves" can handle tough situations, they can, too.

Stories are healing and empowering. They're brain-growing and encouraging. They're rooted in the knowledge that kids can, and do, figure things out and grow up just like the rest of us.

We can give them a head start of making sense of their place in the world and of their relationships with the people around them. And most importantly, these stories can become a part of their inner narrative about who they know themselves to be and what they can offer the world.

Part 4:

TELLING FAMILY STORIES

CHAPTER 18:

CREATING FAMILY VALUES AND IDENTITY

There's another side of story teaching. It comes in a form I call *the family narrative*.

True, for some, telling family stories may conjure images of tales being spun around a campfire. While that's all well and good, personally, I am neither much of a camper nor a fire-builder (although I'm working on both).

Telling family stories—for most of us, anyway—is much more informal than the campfire version. Sometimes, we may not even realize we're storytelling. We simply see our words as relaying information about our family members, talking about our day, or sharing some random experience.

No matter the venue or method (no tent or s'mores required), there's great wisdom in family storytelling, and it has some compelling benefits. First, though, let's look a bit more closely at what family stories are.

What Are Family Stories?

Family stories can be as simple as recounting a shared experience that happened within the child's lifetime and that they remember. An example might be: "Remember that time I accidentally dumped an open bottle of maple syrup on your head while you were sitting at the kitchen table? That was hilarious." (True story. Sometimes I have fabulous parenting skills.)

Alternatively, family stories might also be stories from the child's lifetime, which the child doesn't remember. Example: "I love this rocking chair. I remember holding you when you were a baby and rocking you to sleep. I'd often sit there and hold you for your whole nap. I loved your snuggles. I must've kissed your head a billion times."

Going further back, you might tell stories about family members from deeper in your child's lineage. You might share how your parents met, something funny or challenging that happened to you in school, or anything else that gives your children a glimpse of life before they were born.

Stories about the family's past make you more personal and relatable to your children. Naturally, they see you primarily through the lens of your parenting. Sharing memories about your life before your children were born helps them better understand the big picture of who you are. This, in turn—and especially as your children grow older—can deepen the level of your family's intimacy and understanding of one another.

You might go even further back in your family's history, telling stories about people they never could've met, such as long-gone grandparents. For instance, "Did you know that when your great-granddad served in WWII halfway around the world, he earned a medal of honor for running across a minefield multiple times to save the lives of his wounded comrades? This was one example of his selflessness and caring spirit. It's just the kind of human he was. Although it shows up in different ways, I often see these traits in you."

Why Family Storytelling Matters

When parents tell stories about family history, numerous good things happen. Stories aren't just nice to hear. Much more happens beneath the surface, according to research.

Family Storytelling Gives Kids a Stronger Identity

Hearing about their relatives gives children a feeling of connection to their own personal histories. When children feel like they fit in to the family's narrative, it can benefit their self-esteem.

Research shows that having a family identity is linked with more positive outcomes for kids, including greater resiliency and sense of connection.

Family storytelling doesn't have to be particularly meaningful at the surface. Day-to-day anecdotes in normal conversations serve the same purpose as more intentional interactions. Over time, themes will often emerge. Those themes help children build their identity.

For example, if children repeatedly hear stories about adults in their family who were kind, they may grow up embracing kindness. It's part of what they've learned, one story at a time, about who "their people" are.

What About Problematic Family Narratives?

I'd be remiss if I didn't address tricky family narratives. I don't, even for a second, pretend that life is all rainbows and unicorns—unless you're a child, in which case, for a while, life is predominantly governed by rainbows and unicorns. The rest of us, though, acknowledge the hard stuff. Our families of origin can be messy.

Trust your intuition when it comes to timing and how much to divulge, but it can be healthy for kids to understand some of the less-than-picturesque moments of family history, too. Once again, it's likely much better that they hear about the harder parts of life from you than from some random relative or other person who assumed they knew and told them on your behalf.

An Example:

Although my daughter has always known that some families look very different from ours, she never really questioned why that is. She'd simply accepted that one of her friends lives only with her mom and knows nothing about her dad; another goes back and forth between her parents' homes; and so on across all varieties of family dynamics and living arrangements.

When she was about seven, however, we discussed having her grandma, my mom, drive across the country to visit us. All good, right? Indeed, until she asked whether her granddad would be coming at the same time. That would be a hard *no* for many reasons, not the least of which is that they're divorced.

It apparently never occurred to her that we don't ever see them together, and they never share phone calls with one another, either. Suddenly, though, she wanted to know why I had a visceral reaction at the very idea of them coming to visit at the same time.

This was our foray into discussing the *what* and the *why* of our family history. In age-appropriate ways, we discussed struggles related to family of origin and intergenerational trauma. It also gave me an opportunity to discuss the importance of healthy boundaries, as well as mental health and why I still have therapy appointments sometimes. (I'm a big fan of normalizing therapy. There's no shame in it, and I want my child to feel safe seeking it if she ever wants to.)

The important piece to add here is that when family narratives are tricky, it behooves us to add what we're doing to be healthier, more peaceful, or to gain whatever it is we need. We must discuss ways that empower us to become changemakers and cycle breakers. In doing so, our children don't feel tied to the notion of continuing unhealthy patterns. Tell them what you've done or what you're currently doing to change the family narrative for the better. It's imperative that they know their family history does not need to be their destiny.

Finally, be sure to tell stories that mirror the child's lived experience. The child should be able to see their own family reflected in the stories you relay. Keep in mind that *family* doesn't have to be biological, either. I'm an only child, so I've been intentional about choosing friends of mine to be my daughter's "aunts" and "uncles." These people are a positive influence on her life. Our chosen family can be absolutely as valid as any other.

Needless to say, many of us—okay, *all* of us—have stories and traumas we'd rather not remember. As it turns out, however, telling these stories can be incredibly beneficial in the context of forming a coherent narrative. (For more on this, look to part 5.)

Telling Family Stories Reinforces Values

Telling family stories isn't just about relaying past experiences. It's also about helping the child relate to others from their past so they can carry a part of those people forward into their own lives, regardless of whether they're still living.

An Example:

I once introduced my child to my grandmother's best cookie recipe, which I enjoy baking as a tradition to carry on my grandma's memory.

It's not just about the cookies, though. I told my daughter about what a brave and creative baker her great-grandmother was, rarely using others' recipes and, instead, coming up with delicious concoctions all on her own. Her pumpkin chocolate chip cookies are unrivaled in my world.

My daughter decided that she, too, loves seeing how bravery and creativity can manifest in the kitchen. Now she comes up with culinary combinations I'd never have considered. More than passing on generations of out-of-the-(cookie)-box thinking, she's come to associate bravery and creativity as being part of her identity. She's creating a narrative about herself based on our family history.

Would she be the same person, happily baking alongside me, if she didn't know those were attributes of generations past? Maybe, but I doubt it. Simply by knowing things through family history and stories, her identity and confidence grow.

What about kids who don't recall their early childhood or have family to tell them about their life's beginning?

Not everyone knows their full story or family history. That's okay. Fortunately, we have two good alternatives that still provide significant benefits.

The first is that we can work with what we do know. A client of mine, for example, was adopted when he was very young from a country far away from where he grew up (I'm changing some of his details for privacy). He has virtually no knowledge of his early life. What he does have, however, is his cultural identity.

The more he delves into understanding his birth culture, the more he can piece together what his life might've been like in his early days. He also knows that someone loved him enough to make sure he was well cared for before his adoption, where his known story begins.

He's never going to hear about family memories from his biological parents, nor will his story ever have any of the specific details he craves. However, he's learning to speak the primary language of his country of origin, learning to cook its recipes, and creating a sense of his whole self, even without the details. He can work to create his story even if he's unclear about its specifics.

Second, we have our intuition. Even the seemingly illogical or inexplicable feelings we have still tell us a story about our past. I cover this topic in part 5, "Stories for Healing."

Sometimes we might wonder why we seem to know things that don't seem tied to any of our conscious memories. That's because our bodies carry our history.

Storytelling from the Past: Written Stories

Not all stories need to be oral. Some families also tell stories through writing and pass those memories along through multiple generations. What a gift it is for a child to see the writing of someone in their personal history, noting events they'd never have known otherwise.

Written stories, especially if accompanied by a photo, can help a child form more of a coherent image of their lineage and history, not to mention the inherent romanticism of feeling connected to long-lost relatives.

Perhaps you have a copy of love letters your great-grandparents exchanged, along with some old-time photos of them. This is a powerful peek into the past.

Storytelling for the Future

Some families also enjoy writing letters to their future selves, perhaps in the form of a time capsule. It may include a letter from a mother and father, for example, to their children about how much they love them, or where they guess they'll be later in their lives. These stories may cover an adventure or a dream the family has had, or hopes to have, such as traveling to a faraway land.

It's fun to see later if those plans ever came to fruition.

An Example:

I've been writing my daughter love letters ever since she was an infant. Although I've sometimes taken some long breaks in between letters, it gives me peace to know that someday she'll have a written record of how loved she's been her entire life. I collect them all in the same place—a box I call *the box of love*—and I'll likely give them to her when she's a young adult. She can choose whether to read them then or to wait.

What Family Storytelling Isn't

If you noticed in the examples above, every single one of them, although they were short, had an anchor to an emotion, either implicitly or overtly.

We can have, for example, visceral memories of an event that was hilarious. We may smile or laugh about it years after the fact. If we express a sense of pride or gratitude or joy—or even pain or sadness—those things come out in our storytelling as well.

They don't have to be big events. For example, my daughter loves to remind my husband of the time he accidentally sprinkled pumpkin pie spice all over his meal instead of the turmeric he'd intended. That made for a very different meal from the one he'd been craving. Likewise, she reminds me of the time I accidentally melted our pressure cooker. It wasn't my finest moment, but to her, it's still hilarious; hence, it's a family story. For better or worse, it connects us.

What family storytelling isn't, then, is stories devoid of emotion.

Did you, for example, lose your keys and you're trying to retrace your steps? Okay, then it's helpful. But this "story" certainly is not going to get passed on to the next generation. That's not to say that all stories do get passed along—that's not necessary—but if there's no emotional anchor, this type of story is more or less meaningless.

The key to the art of storytelling, then, is that it connects us to one another emotionally.

Family Activity: Round Robin Storytelling

One of the family activities we enjoy is to make up stories together at the dinner table.

How it works is that someone gives the opening line to the story, and each person adds a line. You end up with all sorts of silliness. It's wonderfully connecting.

For example, I might start the story with this: "Once upon a time, there was a king in the Kingdom of Kingdomhood. One day, he forgot his pants at the palace before he set off to ride his pet dragon."

And then I would pass the story to the next person, who would add a single sentence or event, and then so on around the table.

Not only do children love these stories, but the adults tend to stay actively engaged in them as well.

Best of all, both children and their parents create wonderful memories together.

Alternatively, this is sometimes enjoyable to do as a writing exercise (and great practice for the emergent reader and writer).

Here, the parent or the child may write the first lines of the story on a piece of paper. Then, they pass the paper to the next person to add to the events of the story.

Not only will this help enhance a child's storytelling skills, it also helps improve their language, reading, and writing skills, not to mention nurture creativity. As you already know, the importance of supporting creativity is more important now than ever. These very moments make it fun and not at all a chore (provided that the child wants to engage in it; I'd never force it).

One important tip: when the child creates stories, it's personal for them. It's already just right as it is. The parent's job isn't to suggest more engaging language or make it feel for the child like being corrected in school; that can deter the child from participating.

The point of this activity isn't the "school-ish" part of it. It's about making personal and meaningful memories together. Families connect this way.

We get to say *yes* to our children's stories wherever and whatever they are, because these are our children's stories, born of their hearts. This is the joy and connection they'll pass on through the generations.

Part 5:

STORIES FOR HEALING

CHAPTER 19:

CREATING COHERENT NARRATIVES

Story teaching for healing is an incredibly powerful tool from which adults and children alike can benefit. Storytelling in this form helps us form what's called a *coherent narrative*.

A coherent narrative is how we make sense of the stories we've created for ourselves about the events that have transpired in our lives.

If we can talk about a past event in a fluid, congruent, and logical way, our narrative is coherent. If our story is disjointed, confusing, or missing parts that would be critical to understanding it clearly, our narrative is incoherent.

Why We Want a Coherent Narrative

We sometimes have an incoherent narrative when we've experienced a particularly stressful and/or traumatic event. An example might be an unexpected loss of a loved one or a pet. We may have a sense that we're "all over the place" when we talk about it. We feel disjointed and discombobulated. We may not even be sure how we got to this difficult point in our lives in the first place; we just know we're struggling. It may feel really, incredibly, insurmountably messy.

Conversely, with practice—and sometimes with professional support—we can create a coherent narrative for our stressful or traumatic events. Perhaps we debrief about a stressful situation with a friend or partner; we might journal, pray, or meditate about it. We might work extensively with a therapist, if appropriate. Regardless, we get it out somehow and make sense of what happened.

Regardless of our method and emotional state, many of us have learned from experience that when we can get things off our chest and feel heard, we feel better. When we release our wounds by telling our stories *and* making sense of them, we can gain a greater sense of peace.

Making sense of our stories and forming a coherent narrative helps us heal. This is why it's important to consciously and intentionally process what's happened.

How exactly do we heal, though?

For both adults and children, there's great hope of creating a coherent narrative through intentional storytelling.

Children Need Support to Form a Coherent Narrative

We know that keeping a difficult memory from the past bottled up could negatively affect our present and future well-being. At the same time, we all know the power and importance of healing. Coherence often comes from being able to essentially dissect a memory and make sense of it.

For young children, however, this can be tricky for a variety of reasons.

For starters, children are still developing their sense of self. They're learning where they fit into their family, their school (if they have one), and their place in the community. Their family patterns are just being established for the first time. They lack enough past experience to understand the context of situations and how their ability to process them matters.

"Is my experience normal?" children might wonder. "Does everyone go through what I just did?" As a mere function of their young age, they've not yet had the opportunity to decipher all the patterns and schemas that are essential to understanding how life is supposed to work. Everything is normal to them because it's all they know.

Further, their language skills are not as developed as those of an older child or adult. It's certainly hard to form a coherent narrative if they don't, quite literally, have the words to describe their story.

Moreover, emotional regulation and communication in general are new to them, as is developmentally appropriate. In fact, the part of their brain that's primarily responsible for making sense of situations, helping them plan, and helping them understand the consequences of their actions hasn't even fully matured yet. This part of the brain is called the *prefrontal cortex*, and as you recall, it won't be completely developed until the child is approximately twenty-five years old.

Just because children are young, however, it doesn't mean they're likely to just forget an event of the past and move on from a negative experience. The brain doesn't work that way (as helpful as it might sometimes be if it did).

Subconscious Memories in a Coherent Narrative

As Bessel van der Kolk explains in his book *The Body Keeps the Score*, our bodies do indeed hold on to previous experiences, both negative and positive, both actively remembered and "forgotten."

Interestingly, as we now know from neuroscience, we have not just one type of memory but two: implicit and explicit. Both types of memories are stored in our nervous system in meaningful ways. They can affect our physical and mental health.

Our implicit memories are the ones we don't actively remember. Often, they include experiences from when we were very young. Tina Payne Bryson, PhD, and Daniel J. Siegel, MD, address the concept in their best-selling parenting book *The Whole-Brain Child*. Explicit memories are the ones we consciously remember.

Creating Coherence for Implicit Memories

If you're wondering whether it's possible to heal from and create a coherent narrative for memories we didn't even know we had, the answer is a resounding *yes*.

Whether we, or our children, clearly remember our experiences is, in some ways, of little importance. Of course, it's easier to create a coherent narrative when we have an obvious memory of an event that's transpired. It's not required, however.

Whether for ourselves or for our children, when we experience a feeling for what seems to be "no good reason," we can shift from dismissing the feeling to letting ourselves feel it. We can interpret the feeling as a messenger.

If this feeling had a voice, what would it be saying to us?

As Drs. Siegel and Bryson say, and as I mentioned earlier:

- "Name it to frame it." When we name the emotion we're feeling, it helps minimize its power over us.
- "Feel it to heal it." This means that the most effective way to heal is to allow our feelings rather than to suppress them.

For example, if sadness comes up for you when you walk past a lake you've never wandered past before, you might be inclined to wonder, *Why do I feel sad? It's beautiful here. I need to get over it and distract myself. I should be thankful for this view. What's wrong with me?*

It's quite likely that nothing at all is wrong with you (or perhaps more accurately, there's not more wrong with you than there is most other people). The images in front of you may be triggering something that's entirely out of your control, yet dismissing them won't address your authentic internal experience.

What if, instead, you responded to your sadness in this example with *Hmmm. I feel sad. Sadness, thanks for joining me. I don't know what's bringing you here, but walk with me as long as you need to.* Befriending *all* our feelings, even those that have traditionally made us feel uncomfortable, helps us feel safer with them.

When we feel safer with our feelings, we can hear their messages more clearly.

When we model for our kids that feelings are messengers, we show them that we don't need to run from ourselves emotionally. Instead, we can meet ourselves with compassion and gentleness.

However, we often avoid expressing our anger. It makes sense that we don't want to yell at our kids, for example, if we're trying to parent peacefully. If we end up stuffing down our anger rather than finding a healthy outlet for it, though, we're more likely to eventually explode like a volcano full of angry mama-magma (or your role's equivalent). The key is to let it out in ways that do no harm, such as using the calming tools discussed earlier.

Still, we often want the anger to go away as quickly as possible, to disappear magically somehow. It's uncomfortable. Many of us were discouraged from showing our anger when we were children.

When we reframe anger as a messenger, however, we can get curious about it and ask ourselves things like, "What do I need right now?"

Anger sometimes tells us, for example, that we have an unfulfilled need that only we have the power to provide for ourselves. It may also be telling us that we have some work to do around setting boundaries.

We are responsible for meeting our own needs. This isn't to say we don't need other people, but no other person can ever be singularly responsible for our well-being.

For example, maybe we want a clean house and the mess is triggering for us. At the same time, maybe no one else in our home cares one whit about cleanliness. We can't make them care about cleaning, so we have two options: 1) find peace with the mess, or 2) find a way to make it clean enough to reduce our stress, with or without help from others. If it's our problem, it's our problem and no one else's.

Moreover, allowing ourselves to welcome our feelings rather than suppress them is a key to releasing whatever patterns we've been carrying, even if the patterns are unbeknownst to us. The same is true for our children.

If a child seems to be having an off day for no discernible reason, or is expressing their big feelings in ways that catch us off guard, we can get curious about them. We can hold space for those feelings, as discussed in chapter 4.

We can model for them how to trust and accept their feelings by honoring their emotional experience, whatever it may be. We can help them make friends with their internal lives, to embrace their emotional journey. We can teach them not to run from their feelings but, instead, to welcome the integration of whatever their full experience is telling them.

A child's ability to engage in healthy communication with themselves later (when they're an adult), often rests on their family's ability to welcome all their feelings when they're young. They learn whether their feelings are safe or unsafe, even when those feelings arise for seemingly "no good reason."

A Note About Intergenerational Trauma

Trauma doesn't have to have happened directly to us for it to be significant. Beyond subconscious memories from our own lives, intergenerational trauma may come into play as well. Intergenerational trauma is defined as:

> trauma that gets passed down from those who directly experience an incident to subsequent generations. Intergenerational trauma may begin with a traumatic event affecting an individual, traumatic events affecting multiple family members, or collective trauma affecting larger community, cultural, racial, ethnic, or other groups/populations (historical trauma).[45]

An example might be a grandfather who experienced trauma by being on the front lines of a war; his stress may be carried on in future generations, even though his grandchildren weren't pres-

45 Fabiana Franco, "Understanding Intergenerational Trauma: An Introduction for Clinicians," Good Therapy, January 8, 2021, https://www.goodtherapy.org/blog/Understanding_Intergenerational_Trauma.

ent during the battles.

It's important to process whatever feeling comes up simply by allowing yourself to feel it, even if the triggering event doesn't seem related to whatever feelings are arising.

It may not be our "stuff," but it might just be our stuff to heal.

Creating a Coherent Narrative for Explicit Memories

When we directly remember experiences that need processing, one of the easiest ways to create a coherent narrative is to replay the events in question in emotionally safe ways. We can use language that helps form healing memories about whatever's happened and provides the emotional tools to deal with them.

I'll share a true story (as all stories in this book are) of a recent day in my life with my husband and child. I'll share the same story twice; once with the event in factual terms without much of a coherent narrative, and again with narratives that helped my child know what to do with the information. As the adult doing the explaining, I also benefit from making sense of the story.

The Event Without a Coherent Narrative

Our family drove up a mountain. We got lost, and it hailed, and my husband lost his wedding ring. It was my birthday, and the car wouldn't start, and it was awful.

What in the world just happened? It sounds rather negative and all over the place, doesn't it? It's just a string of bad news with a random mention of my birthday thrown in.

If my child and I stayed with this as our narrative, it's not likely that we'd have a healthy or peaceful memory of that day. It started off disjointed, and it ends up staying that way.

Even worse than telling this version of the story is if I say nothing. If I say nothing to my child about the day, we both lack the opportunity to form a coherent narrative around it. The bad day simply stays a bad day. There's no story to make it better; it just lives on in blah-land.

The Event with a Meaningful, Coherent Narrative

On my birthday this year, our family drove up a mountain to go hiking. It was such an adventure! We didn't realize we'd need a reservation, so when we reached the top of the mountain, we were turned away by the forest ranger at the welcome center. Unfortunately, there was no Internet access at the top of the mountain, but it was easy enough to drive back down the mountain and get Internet access. When we drove back down, we were able to get a same-day reservation. I'm so thankful we didn't have to cancel our plans!

We waited only an hour for our allotted time slot once we were back at the top, which was the perfect amount of time for us to have lunch and stretch our legs a bit before the hike. Waiting turned out to be a gift because a hailstorm started, and we were still close enough to take cover in the car rather than being hailed on out in the wilderness.

Once the hail stopped, we started on our hike, only to realize that we'd taken a longer trail than we needed to take. On the bright side, it was more exercise and more time in nature—called *forest bathing*—so doubly beneficial! The scenery was incredible, and we all felt so connected.

Toward the end of our hike, we had a surprise visitor—a spider fell down from a tree and landed inside the back of my husband's shirt! When my husband grabbed the spider and tried to wildly shake it off his hand, he accidentally catapulted his wedding ring into the wilderness. If there's a bright side there, it's that our ten-year-anniversary is coming up and we've been renewing and healing our marriage. The opportunity for him to get a new ring later this year will be the perfect way to celebrate the healthy changes we've made.

Once we got back to the car, we realized the battery in my key fob had died and my car didn't start. With some creative thinking by the forest ranger and my husband, however, we found a way to start the car and drive back home. Plus, rather than having to throw together a rushed dinner, it was a good excuse to stop at the new pizza place I've been eyeing. Overall, despite its challenges, it was one of my favorite birthdays ever.

What changed?

As you likely noticed in this coherent narrative,

- The story is much more fluid
- I've used emotionally positive terms for my child and me to attach to our memory of the day
- For my child's and my own mental health, I've opted to suggest focusing on the positive aspects of the negative events that transpired that day

Making sense of our story in positive ways not only creates a coherent narrative, but it also offers us significant opportunities to see the good in all situations—the silver lining, as it were.

To be clear, a coherent narrative doesn't have to have a happy ending. I choose to add positivity because it helps remind children of their resiliency. The more kids practice witnessing and acknowledging their own resiliency, the more naturally their brains reinforce seeing it reappear in other situations.

Further Support for Children's Coherent Narrative

The more attuned an adult is to their child's inner world, the more they can help them create a coherent narrative that's free from the adult's narrative and unintentional biases. It's not always about the adult's coherence; it's about relaying accurate information *from the child's perspective.*

Why should the story be about their perspective rather than others' experience? If you recall from earlier in this book when I covered attention-seeking behavior, you learned that children are naturally self-centered. It's how they're supposed to be until their brains grow a bit more. Their brains focus on the experience of the "self" to keep them physically and emotionally safe.

For example, let's say a child witnesses their parents arguing. A coherent narrative for one or both of the adults might include why they were arguing and what each of them brought into the heated discussion.

The child might not benefit from this being part of their coherent narrative. It might not make sense to them, and it does nothing to strengthen their inner sense of safety. Instead, the child's version of a coherent narrative might sound something like this, as explained to the child by the parent:

"You saw Mommy and Daddy yelling at each other. Mommy got upset and threw down the pen she was holding. That made Daddy jump. When that happened, it was scary for you because you didn't know what was going to happen. Then, Mommy calmed down and apologized. Daddy accepted her apology, and then they hugged. Now they're peaceful again."

Here, not only is the story accurate from the child's point of view, but the adult is clearly attuned to the child's unique perspective. Attunement helps children feel seen and validated. When the child feels seen and validated, they feel safer.

Children need to feel that they're not alone; that someone gets their experience. A successful and coherent narrative results in "My feelings make sense. I make sense exactly as I am." Validation like this can offer children incredible emotional safety.

To be clear, we can absolutely tell stories that encourage perspective taking. Taking others' perspectives is an important life skill. However, a coherent narrative is work we do to heal ourselves—not others—hence my focus here.

Whatever story we tell children about their relationships and experiences, including those that they don't explicitly remember, is the story they'll carry forward through life. They'll have their own opinions about it, too, of course.

An Example:

One day, not long ago, I got food poisoning. (I give food poisoning zero stars.) It passed quickly, but my daughter went from seeing me fine one minute to violently ill the next. Fortunately, the worst of it was over quickly.

Before I moved on with our day, I paused, looked her in the eye, and said, "I bet it was scary to see me get so sick unexpectedly."

Although she'd been smiling before I said that, her tears suddenly burst forth the moment those words left my lips. She nodded and said, "Yes, I was really scared."

I chose to be proactive about naming her feelings because I knew she had to have been frightened. Pretending she wasn't, and moving on, would've left that stress in her system. I wanted to give her an outlet for her fear.

We talked through how and why my food poisoning happened, how she and Daddy took good care of me while I was ill, and how her love helped me heal. I told her that the story she read to me while I was lying in bed holding my tummy instantly helped me feel better. She got to see herself as a helper, and she heard—and witnessed—that Mama is all better now.

Having this coherent narrative helped her heal from this scary situation. It released the stress she'll no longer have to carry.

Creating a Coherent Narrative Offers Protective Benefits

As it turns out, we don't just feel better when we tell our stories to others. This storytelling is deeply healing and beneficial.

"Narrating about personal experiences in a coherent manner is . . . beneficial for one's well-being."[46] Specifically, according to the research of Daniel J. Siegel and other mental health experts,

46 Louise Vanden Poel and Dirk Hermans, "Narrative Coherence and Identity: Associations with Psychological Well-Being and Internalizing Symptoms," Frontiers in Psychology, Frontiers, May 24, 2019, https://www.frontiersin.org/articles/10.3389/fpsyg.2019.01171/full.

creating a coherent narrative can be a key to integration, or a fully embodied acceptance, of our stories. This integration can be instrumental in

- Reducing trauma
- Promoting healing
- Improving mental health
- Breaking damaging cycles
- Finding more joy in life

These narratives don't just have to be recent events, above and beyond intergenerational trauma as covered earlier. Creating a coherent narrative around events that have long since happened in our own lives—even those from years ago—can still offer protective benefits. In other words, it's never too late to heal.

As an example of the long-standing opportunity for healing, in his online interpersonal neurobiology course, Dr. Daniel J. Siegel shares a story of a ninety-two-year-old man who finally heals from childhood trauma. He was able to reset relationships that had suffered for almost a century.

The brain holds our memories for as long as we need to process them. And when we process them with a coherent narrative, we can heal.

Needless to say, releasing our early traumatic experiences as soon as possible and allowing ourselves to heal is better than harboring long-term stress and trauma.

However, it's never too late to create a coherent narrative and benefit from the healing process. We can do this work for ourselves and alongside our children. From this work, everyone in our inner world is better for our healing journey. And it all starts with making sense of a story.

CHAPTER 20:

HELPING KIDS TELL THEIR OWN STORIES

Not all storytelling needs to be adult-led. In fact, sometimes it's more healing for the child if they author or coauthor the tale, with or without an adult in tow.

Just as it's helpful for an adult to form a coherent narrative about events that have transpired in their own lives, kids can lead the action, too. It's empowering for them.

What does this look like in action? Here are a few ideas.

A young child who can't yet read or write can still express their feelings in written form. How? An adult can help the child befriend paper and a writing instrument to express themselves.

If the child is amid a big emotional release, some children will benefit from the adult saying, "Yes! I welcome your big feelings here! They're safe with me. Let's draw what they look like and get them out on paper!"

The adult then hands the child a crayon / some finger paint / whatever's safe (and ideally washable!) and co-regulates with the child through drawing. Some call this an informal version of art therapy. Art therapy with a trained therapist can be really beneficial, too.

How does the adult co-regulate with the child? This happens a few ways:

1. By helping the child name their emotion or taking a guess on the child's behalf, typically saying something along the lines of, "I hear that you're feeling angry" (if the child has named it), or "I'm wondering if you're feeling angry."

2. By validating the child's emotion and allowing space for it.
3. By allowing the child to express it fully and without being guided to feel something different before they're ready (i.e., no drawing smiley faces while the child is crying).
4. By staying with the child and supporting them at their own pace until the emotional storm has passed.

In step 1, before proceeding, the adult waits for validation or correction. As you recall, this is part of emotion coaching. Once the adult nails it (or better, if the child self-identifies the emotion—although that's not to be expected of young children), the adult can add, "Let's see what mad looks like on paper!" The adult might demonstrate by drawing big, angry scribbles across the page. They might not look like anything recognizable. Anger can be messy, literally and figuratively.

Of course, you can expand this therapeutic assignment to include a verbal story and/or a visual story to help the child process the details of what's happened, above and beyond drawing the emotion.

For instance, you might say, "When I got home from work today and was grouchy, I bet my yelling sounded like a lion's roar. Did my roaring seem big and scary to you? Let's draw what I looked like to you. What kind of animal did you feel like? A tiny mouse? Okay. Let's draw you, too. Great!"

When the child is a bit calmer, the adult might continue, "Now that we see this on paper, let's draw how it felt when I apologized, and we started hugging."

It doesn't have to take much time or paper, especially if you're dealing with a child who has a short attention span, but odds are good that they'll stay engaged as long as they're processing and feeling seen. To be clear, it also takes absolutely zero art skills. Stick-figure lions and whatnot work fine.

Whenever possible, try to get to the phase where the child can draw how they felt after the problem was resolved. That will help ground them in their sense of inner safety. If that doesn't happen, however, and the child has already moved on, you've already done the most important part: you've helped them "name it to frame it."

A Note About Timing

Naturally, it's helpful to the child if the adult doesn't save introducing and practicing this exercise for when the child has already gone off the proverbial rails. It's much easier to model this exercise when all is right with the world.

Ideally, the adult will have modeled something like "I'm feeling happy and peaceful right now. You are, too? Great! Let's draw a picture of what our feelings look like. Let's draw a scene from a time when we felt this way." Perhaps you end up with a picture at the beach, at a playground, or simply holding hands. (Let me reiterate: no art skills are required.)

That way, when things get inevitably bumpy some other time, this whole paper-crayon-feelings business isn't going to make your child give you the side-eye.

This is, indeed, visual storytelling. It counts!

Alternatively, you and your child can practice drawing the trickier feelings on paper when everyone's regulated and calm.

Why on earth would you invite your child to draw mad/sad/scared/disgusted when they're calm and peaceful? Isn't that asking for trouble?

Perhaps surprisingly, children—like all of us—have a need to find emotional safety in situations that might otherwise feel overwhelming to them. It's part of the reason some children are seemingly drawn to big feelings—these emotions are fascinating to the developing brain!

In fact, there's no better time to discuss (or draw) these trickier emotions than when the child can process them a bit more objectively. Does that mean you draw something terrifying for them? Goodness, no. It does, however, reinforce that all their feelings are safe here (sound familiar?) because we've created the safest possible environment in which to explore these feelings. Just like we sometimes bottle up our emotions, our children sometimes have unresolved feelings, and expressing them through a safe outlet helps to relieve children of the burden of carrying them around.

My only word of caution here is to stay present with your child as they do this work; continual co-regulation is what creates this sense of safety within the context of things that feel less safe to them. You're there to help ground them. This is especially important for highly sensitive children. They need you to be their rock when they're practicing what are sometimes overwhelming emotions for them, even if those emotions are happening in others and/or fictionally.

If the child isn't into drawing, you can find lots of preprinted products that show emotions called *feelings cards*—or better, you can make homemade versions. I made a version at home that was a simple sheet of paper divided into the six primary emotions. It looked something like this:

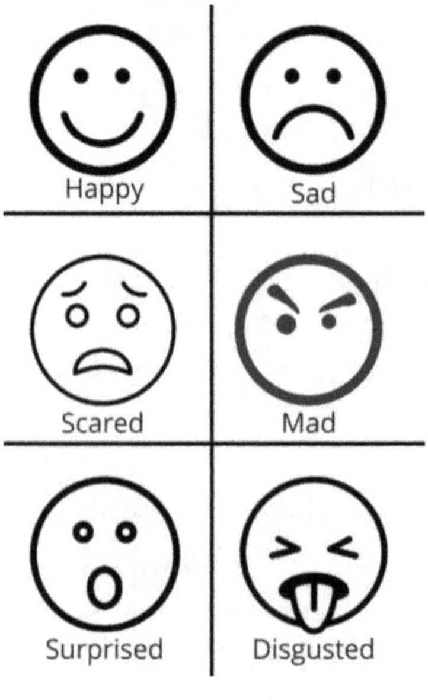

When my child was little and struggling to name her emotional experience in words, sometimes she'd simply walk over and point to the one that resonated most strongly with her. It was immensely helpful for me in moments when I felt like a bewildered mama!

I also added some pictures that indicated things like *tired* so that she could tell me without having to say it. Only twice in her life did she ever say, "Mama, I'm tired. Can I please go take a nap?" Both times, I basically peeled myself off the floor and was happy to oblige for She Who Stayed Awake Seemingly 24/7.

Once our basic version of art therapy took hold, she'd sometimes be proactive about drawing her feelings. It felt emotionally safe for her to do so. More than once did I feel it was the precursor to journaling, without having to teach her to journal!

Finger Play and Story Teaching

Finger play is a very effective way to engage young children in crafting their own stories. In this model, the adult uses their fingers as characters who "talk" to each other and/or to the child. It's wildly fun for little ones.

An Example:

I clearly remember being about five years old, sitting on top of a stack of phone books in the front seat of my mom's big Buick. Since this was in the late 1970s, phone books and front-seat riding were commonplace for kids. Safety hadn't been invented yet.

I don't know whether I was bemoaning the car ride or if Mom was just feeling playful, but suddenly, her right hand—the one closest to me—came off the steering wheel. Rather than acting as "human seat belt" (as was often the case for children who were riding on phone books), she popped her index and middle fingers down to the console between us. They looked like legs on a very small person.

Her fingers started "walking" around on the console and talking to me, playing with me. I was transfixed.

These two little finger-made legs came to be known as "Little Albert," a character I'd know well throughout my childhood.

This Little Albert she invented became my automobile companion and source of entertainment. Her fingers became some of my first real-to-me friends. Being fingers, they were, of course, completely portable and readily available. All we needed were our imaginations.

Although Little Albert took a hiatus for many years in between my own childhood and the birth of my daughter, he never roamed very far. And when the time was right—on my child's first long-haul airplane ride as we moved across the country—I brought Little Albert back to play with her. Sure, he was my own two fingers now and not my mom's, but he worked just the same.

Much to my surprise, however, my child changed how we played the game. I'd never thought to use my own little fingers as characters in response to my mom's. My child, however, embraced the game and added two "Alberts" of her own, which she promptly named Little Chocolate and Little Vanilla. "Albert" became the family surname. Between her two hands, my two, and my husband's two, we suddenly had a whole family of Alberts at the ready for impromptu games.

One of the most fascinating turns of events was that my daughter didn't just want to be entertained by the Alberts. She wanted them to engage with one another, to problem-solve, and to learn how life worked. Protagonists and antagonists evolved in our stories together. They faced challenges and overcame them together. They celebrated together. Each developed its own distinct personality.

These events, and others like them, helped solidify the presence of storytelling in our life. I realized that my daughter was yearning to learn in ways that felt emotionally safe to her. She wanted to process things that had already happened—and prepare for those that hadn't.

She craved gentle correction, guidance, and loving boundaries. In short, she wanted a story road map for life. (Don't we all!)

As I write this, she's eight years old. Although we no longer engage in finger play as we used to, she still asks for Albert stories on a regular basis. Her "sign" (although she's also verbal) is to walk her fingers in the air for a moment. That's my cue to start talking.

To be sure, the Alberts have evolved significantly. Her personality is generally one of risk avoidance and observation, yet she specifically asks for stories where one of the Alberts—Little Garlic, to be specific—misbehaves, takes unfathomable risks, and pushes boundaries. She explores the world through his metaphorical eyes.

Do I tell her these stories to encourage her to misbehave and take wild risks? Of course not. How it works is that she feels safer taking minor risks, being braver than before, and judging right from wrong. Little Garlic is the perfect model for how *not* to live life. What a wonderful teacher to have!

Plus, at her age, she now often gives me the plotline. She tells me exactly what kind of trouble she wants Little Garlic to get into and how the story will evolve. It's worked wonders for supporting her creativity and her own storytelling ability.

This is a life skill that started with a couple of fingers in an old Buick more than forty years ago, and I'd hazard a guess that it'll continue to the next generation, if my daughter has children of her own someday.

Once children are a bit older, you have more options. That said, drawing pictures and various forms of finger play (as I just described above) do not expire at a certain age. Heck, storytelling through art therapy and fantasy is for adults, too! If it keeps working into infinity, why try to change it?

At some point, however, the non-visual-artist child may be ready for more words than pictures or some combination thereof.

For an early reader, you might create a template for them. It could look something like this:

Left side of page: Blank, with instructions to draw what they're feeling.

Draw what you're feeling here. What happened?

Circle the matching feeling:

Happy

Sad

Mad

Scared

Surprised

Disgusted

Frustrated

Silly

Playful

Right side of page: Instructional text, such as "Circle what you feel."

You could also do it as a fill-in-the-blank, depending on whether your child prefers pictures or words.

If it's a fill-in-the-blank, it might look like this:

Here's what happened today:

____

____

____

____

____

____

____

____

____

____

____

When it happened, I felt

____

____

Here's how I got that feeling out:

____

____

Here's who I could talk to about it:

____

____

Here's how I felt after I got it out:

____

____

Additionally, stuffed animals can be your allies here. If you ask your child, "What did you think about your new babysitter today?" your child may or may not open up to you, depending on a number of factors.

To be clear, reluctance to share an experience doesn't necessarily mean that anything bad happened. Some kids just don't always feel like talking about what happened earlier, especially if they've moved on to other activities. They may not feel the need to process experiences as we do. Our curiosity may be greater than their need to divulge the details of their day.

A more engaging way to ask, which may result in a more candid answer, is: "I'm curious what your favorite stuffed animal had to say about the babysitter's visit today."

The child who might've been reluctant to share their own experience might very well have a story to share from the stuffed animal's perspective. Once again, play is very much the language of childhood.

If the child starts to open up, feel free to ask them more questions about the stuffed animal's experience until that well runs dry. The only way nearly guaranteed to make the child clam up again is to forget this discussion is about the stuffed animal (to your child) and suddenly catch your child off guard by being too direct with them. Sometimes the indirect approach feels to the child like the safest way to tell the story.

As an aside, the stuffed animal approach sometimes works well for slightly older children, too. If your child still plays with stuffed animals, regardless of their age, it's likely worth a try. At the same time, we can also be mindful and respectful of our children's decisions not to talk to us about every detail of their lives.

Quick note about safety: If your intuition tells you that something happened that makes you uncomfortable and your child won't talk about it, do explore it. In this case, it may be wise to engage a professional play therapist or other expert support.

Once the child is well versed in writing and/or drawing pictures, a great next step is to give them a diary. This is their place to tell *their* stories: their own versions of them, from their own perspectives, without outside influence or opinion. A powerful place, yes?

Here's the thing, though. The diary, by definition, is private. When giving the child the diary, some adults will say, "This is a diary. It's for you to write in—whatever you want, and especially when you're feeling something that you want to process. Getting your experiences and feelings down on paper is a healthy thing to do. You can either keep it to yourself and know that it's just for you—I trust you and will respect your privacy—or you can share part or all with me or another adult you trust."

Why "another adult" rather than "another person"? Well, I can tell you from firsthand experience what it's like to show another child a diary and have that child repeat the intimate contents of said diary to eager listeners on the playground. Certainly, most kids are trustworthy, and most are still learning what *trustworthy* and *private* mean. (Some adults still struggle with this, after all.)

That's not to say a child shouldn't have a best friend (or friends) with whom they share their heart. It's simply common sense to give your child a heads-up that they should be choosy about the details of their sharing.

Plus, a trustworthy adult will know whether the content requires any sort of intervention, professional or otherwise.

Some adults also take the emphasis off writing "big things to process" and tone it down to "journaling whatever you want to" in the diary. Making it low-key can make it a safer experiment for the child to try, especially if they've never been much for expressing themselves in writing. We don't need to inadvertently pressure them into thinking they can only write "important" things in their diary. Who decides what's "important," anyway?

An Example:

My daughter, age eight, divulged to me that her diary largely consists of drawings she made about that one time our toilet overflowed. It's full of her drawings of me looking frantic and plunging and running to get more towels. These are the memories that are noteworthy to her now, and I can only hope she finds humor in them when she looks back at them someday. It's not mine to judge or suggest that she record anything to the contrary!

Back to the piece about the diary being private. This is worth exploring, too.

When Should Diaries Be Private?

I get it. We really, really want to know the inner workings of our children's hearts and minds—especially if they're not forthcoming enough to tell us all the things. We may feel curious. We may even start to imagine things we'd rather not:

Maybe they're struggling with something?

Maybe they need help in some way?

Maybe (gasp!) they don't like us?

The more energy we put into worrying about what might be in that diary, the more prone we are to catastrophizing. Suddenly, not only do they not like us, they're planning to run away to some exotic island and do nothing with their life but enjoy umbrella drinks on a sunny beach and have sordid affairs with the bronzed locals.

And darn it, they're only ten years old, and that was *our* fantasy. No fair!

See how easy it is for our minds to carry us into places that, when we stop to really think about them, don't make a lot of sense?

In short, diaries need to be private almost all the time. Plus, I daresay that if our child finds out that we've been snooping around—even in their "best interest"—it's going to do us no favors to encourage them to really open up to us.

They will, instead, feel violated. Why? Because we have, in fact, violated their trust. Ouch. Not only will they be more likely to do a better job of locking up their diary, but they're also more likely to further lock up their heart. Backfire. So, when shouldn't diaries be private?

As I've just pointed out, most of the time, diaries should be private. However, there are times when they shouldn't—namely, when you have a specific reason to be genuinely and urgently concerned about your child, and/or if someone has alerted you that your child or someone your child knows may be in danger.

If we've done our due diligence, or the situation comes up with a degree of urgency or importance that doesn't lend itself to waiting awhile and/or attempting other ways to connect with your child, then trust your instincts. I believe in *better safe than sorry*.

A better option than searching their diary, if you fear your child is in danger, is to enlist the immediate support of a trusted counselor, reputable clergy, or someone else who can genuinely help. This person probably isn't your next-door neighbor who "raised three children and knows a lot." Instead, it's likely someone who's specifically trained to address potential crisis situations.

You know your child best. Trust your gut. Reading the diary likely won't be the answer, but getting your child professional help might be.

How Do You Get Your Child to Open Up to You with Their Stories?

I confess this is something of a trick question. We can't "get" them to do that. To the contrary, we need to create a space where they feel emotionally safe and brave enough to do it of their own volition.

Best-case scenario, we start when they're very young by using peaceful discipline from the get-go. We want to nurture an environment so that when someone says to our child, "I'm going to call your mom/dad/caregiver and tell them what you did!" the child's inner response is, "Thank goodness. They can help with whatever's happening here."

Peaceful discipline naturally fosters this emotional environment. If kids know we're on their side, and that they're not going to be "in trouble" for leaning on us even in challenging moments, they grow up in this knowledge.

This doesn't mean every child will divulge everything every single time there's a hiccup or a big problem. In fact, as children grow older, it's developmentally normal for them to tell us less than they used to. It's part of their ever-expanding sense of autonomy. Ultimately, it's what helps them to feel emotionally prepared to move out on their own someday.

However, if the foundation of trust has been laid in the early years, these older children—who become tweens—who become teens—who become young adults—will feel safer to tell us the big stuff *and* the small stuff than those who fear our reaction (or worry that we don't care enough to react at all). They will want to lean into us more.

I have good news for you even if you didn't start out using peaceful discipline—it's not too late.

You might be wondering, *How the heck does she know it's not too late? She doesn't even know how old my child is or how long we've been struggling!*

You're right. I have no idea whose hands this book is in right now, and I don't know your story. What I do know is this: healing is possible.

Sometimes, children who've never felt heard or seen or validated because their parents were controlling and oppressive start to heal because, one day, one of those adults decides to listen. *Really listen.*

With empathetic listening from the adult—without shaming, judging, or even fixing—the door to healing can start to creak its way open. To be sure, sometimes families need a highly skilled therapist or other support to help them open this door further and prevent it from slamming shut in their faces. I don't mean to imply that this is always easy work.

With time, practice, and support, children can start to feel safer telling their stories—because we make it safe for them to do so.

Here's the thing, though. Some kids will never open up to us completely about everything. As hard as it is for us to reconcile that (especially when we really, really want to be their "safe person"), what matters more than them telling us their stories is that they have a reliable, mature, trustworthy person in whom to potentially confide.

Research tells us that children need exactly *one* adult in whom they can trust, confide, and rest emotionally in order to thrive.[47] Sure, they can have more, but they don't need more than one. We often inherently understand this as adults: we have that one friend or partner with whom we feel totally safe. Maybe we have more, but we know above all that we have "our person."

It may be helpful to think back to when you were a child. Who was your special person—someone you trusted completely—if you had one? What qualities did they possess? How did they create a sense of safety for you? Odds are good that if you felt peaceful with them, they somehow showed up for you in a way that was consistent and predictable (even if you didn't speak with them often).

If you didn't have that one person when you were a child, can you imagine the type of person you'd have wanted to open up to? What qualities would that person have possessed? What were you needing more than anything from a listener when you were younger? Odds are good that whatever you needed then, you still need now.

By the time I was an adult, one of the most important people in my life was my granddad. I didn't necessarily tell him every-

47 Tina Payne Bryson and Daniel J. Siegel, *The Power of Showing Up*, (New York: Ballantine Books, 2020).

thing that was going on in my life, but I did know that every time I called him, I'd come out of that conversation feeling lighter and more joyful. He was kind to me, and perhaps more than anything, he sounded deeply interested in whatever I had to tell him, no matter how mundane it was. I must've provided some of that to him, too, because I ended up being the one person he shared the most stories with about his time as a spy in World War II (in an organization called the OSS, which was the precursor to the CIA); along with many other details of his life he hadn't shared elsewhere.

Somehow, it didn't matter what else I had going on in my life. Simply being in his presence, even over the phone, reassured me that everything was going to turn out all right.

When children have that one person, they feel safe to tell their stories and to create a secure attachment to their own lives. That's the goal of every life story: to produce children who know, "My story makes sense, and therefore, I make sense—just as I am."

Part 6:

SAMPLE STORIES

In this section, I offer sample stories for common challenges that parents and children face. It's important to note that some struggles are very developmentally appropriate for young children and stories won't necessarily "solve" them. We can't make children's brains mature faster. However, with story teaching, we can facilitate the learning process.

I've intentionally included rich and descriptive vocabulary words in most of these stories. Feel free to change whatever you need so that the stories resonate with your child. Using the first story as an example, I've shared two versions of it so you can see how it might change with plainer vocabulary. Adapt as necessary!

Of course, you can also change names, genders, and as many details as you'd like. These are simply a starting point to illustrate the process.

I've also modeled varying degrees of complexity and creativity in the plotlines and characters.

You'll note I've also included the key components of story teaching so you can see how they weave together to make a cohesive narrative for your child, and I've addressed the pieces that are critical to a story's ability to teach. As a reminder, these include:

- Introduction (usually only one or two characters, setting, and a peaceful vibe)
- Problem concept
- Emotion coaching (part 1)
- Resolution
- Emotion coaching (part 2)

Make them your own as you interact with your children, lingering and expanding on the parts that pique their interest, or changing other parts that don't suit them. You can even involve your children and help strengthen their executive function skills by asking what you think the characters should do next. Try the stories with your children directing the plotlines and see how new twists and turns unfold naturally. Most of all, have fun with them. May they bring you joy and connection!

Bodily Care: The Teeth That Would Not Be Brushed (Rich Vocabulary Version)

This is an example of a story that addresses a onetime or recurring problem.

Introduction

Once upon a time, three teeth lived happily inside a child's mouth-cave. Each of the teeth had its own name: the two on the bottom were Kitten Elizabeth and Wonky Petonky. The one on top simply went by Josephine Kerfufflefluff.

All was well in the mouth of teeth. They enjoyed the dark and cozy home that felt so comfortable to them. They generally preferred to rest there undisturbed, except for a bit of growing and shifting here and there.

One day, however, a great light entered the mouth-cave. Suddenly, they saw their reflections in what they'd later learn was called a *mirror*.

Problem concept

As they stood wide-eyed staring at themselves, something positively terrible happened. A gigantic handheld toothbrushing machine approached them and started scrubbing them with cold water and some scratchy back-and-forth motion.

Kitten Elizabeth and Wonky Petonky held on to each other for dear life. They tried to protest, but with every attempt to speak, they were met with more of that cold brushy water. They tried to run but quickly realized they were quite stuck in place. Oh no! What could they do?

Emotion coaching (part 1)

Kitten Elizabeth felt scared. Wonky Petonky felt mad. Neither one of them liked it one bit.

Quickly, they enlisted the help of their good friend Tongue, begging it to cover them up and protect them.

Josephine Kerfufflefluff, being unaware of her friends' distress, continued to gaze onward toward the beautiful light and her shining, sparkling reflection in the mirror. She noticed how with each brush, she was looking lovelier and lovelier. The blueberry bonnet she'd been unable to remove suddenly washed right off her, revealing even more of her glory. The more the strange brushing motion continued, the more fantastic she felt. Gazing longingly at herself, she realized she might just . . . be in love.

When the brushing was done, Josephine Kerfufflefluff rushed to tell her dear friends Kitten Elizabeth and Wonky

Petonky about the incredible experience she'd just had.

"Friends!" she cried excitedly.

Kitten Elizabeth and Wonky Petonky peeked out from their hiding place. "Is it safe?" they asked.

"Oh, my!" she replied, almost bashfully. "Not only is it safe, do you see how glorious I look? Well, it's only half as wonderful as I feel!" And with that, she broke into song about the sense of joy and peace she felt being fully refreshed.

"But wasn't the water cold?" Kitten Elizabeth and Wonky Petonky asked dubiously.

"Hmmm," Josephine Kerfufflefluff responded thoughtfully, "I didn't really notice. Actually, I found it refreshing. I mean, it isn't as if they were using ice cubes. It was cool and beautiful, and if anything, it helped me to feel more sparkly inside and out."

"But wasn't the water wet?" Kitten Elizabeth and Wonky Petonky inquired, raising one eyebrow each.

"Well, it was wet. However, if you think about it, our mouth-cave is rather wet all the time, isn't it? I didn't really mind; in fact, this wetness tasted cleaner somehow. I feel like a whole new tooth. Clean. Refreshed. Stronger . . . empowered. Like I could eat a bowlful of berries and no longer be bothered by the sticky parts. This brushing thing helps me feel good!"

"Wait!" Kitten Elizabeth and Wonky Petonky implored. "Brushing! Didn't it feel too *unsettling*?"

"Oh, not at all," Josephine Kerfufflefluff responded reassuringly. "It felt like a massage or good old-fashioned back scratch. I found it to be entirely relaxing. I sure wish you'd been there. Hey, I have an idea! If it ever happens again, would you try it with me?"

Kitten Elizabeth and Wonky Petonky hesitated. Wonky Petonky, after a long pause, offered, "Well, *maybe*. But I reserve the right to hide under Tongue again if things start to get out of hand. Also, I want to know when it'll be over. I don't want it to go on forever."

"Deal," she replied.

Resolution

Sure enough, the next morning, it happened again. As soon as the light appeared and the toothbrush-tool started advancing in their direction, Josephine Kerfufflefluff said to her friends, "Okay. It's time. Let's take a deep belly breath and prepare for the cool, refreshing water to wash us. It'll be over by the time they're done singing that A-B-C song, whatever *that* is."

Kitten Elizabeth and Wonky Petonky closed their eyes. They imagined what was coming, and when it did, it wasn't as much of a surprise. Also, they knew it was temporary. Wonky even started to feel herself swaying back and forth a bit with the movement of the brush as if she were dancing. They liked it!

When it was all over, dark, calm, and quiet again, the three teeth reconvened. Excitedly, Kitten Elizabeth and Wonky Petonky announced, "Josephine! Whoa! That felt good! The water was a little warmer this time, and we didn't need to hide! We feel squeaky clean and better than we've felt in months! More! More!"

Emotion coaching (part 2)

"I feel calm and peaceful!" announced Kitten Elizabeth.

"I feel happy and refreshed!" added Wonky Petonky.

And so, with great anticipation, the three teeth spent most of their time every day waiting for the Great Brushing Dance, as they'd come to call it. Sure, they enjoyed all the chewing and eating and so forth, but when they went to sleep every night, they all agreed that they felt their most brilliant when they were clean—and they couldn't wait until next time. Finally, the toothbrush was their friend.

The End.

Bodily Care: The Teeth That Would Not Be Brushed (Plain Vocabulary Version)

Introduction

Once upon a time, three teeth lived happily inside a child's mouth-cave. Each of the teeth had its own name: the two on the bottom were Kitten Elizabeth and Wonky Petonky. The one on top simply went by Josephine Kerfufflefluff.

All was well in the mouth of teeth. They enjoyed the dark and cozy home that felt so comfortable to them.

One day, however, the mouth where they lived opened, and they saw a great light. They saw their reflections in what they'd learn was called a *mirror*.

Problem concept

As they stood staring at themselves, a toothbrush entered the mouth and started scrubbing them with cold water and some scratchy brushing motion.

Kitten Elizabeth and Wonky Petonky weren't sure they liked the toothbrush. They tried to hide under their friend Tongue.

Emotion coaching (part 1)

Josephine Kerfufflefluff, however, liked the toothbrush and the cold water. She noticed how with each brush, she was prettier and shinier. The blueberry she'd been unable to remove suddenly washed right off. She felt happy!

She told her friends how good and clean she felt.

"But wasn't the water cold?" Kitten Elizabeth and Wonky Petonky asked.

"Hmmm," Josephine Kerfufflefluff responded. "No, not too cold."

"But wasn't the water wet?" Kitten Elizabeth and Wonky Petonky asked, raising one eyebrow each.

"Well, it was wet. However, if you think about it, our mouth is rather wet all the time, isn't it? I didn't really mind; in fact, this wetness tasted *cleaner* somehow. This brushing thing helps me feel good! Would you try it with me sometime?"

Kitten Elizabeth and Wonky Petonky said yes.

Resolution

Sure enough, the next morning, the toothbrush entered the mouth again. Josephine Kerfufflefluff said to her friends, "Okay. It's time. Let's take a deep belly breath and prepare for the cool, refreshing water to wash us. It'll be over by the time they're done singing that A-B-C song, whatever *that* is."

Kitten Elizabeth and Wonky Petonky closed their eyes. They imagined what was coming, and when it did, it wasn't as much of a surprise. Also, they knew it was temporary—it would be over soon. They liked it!

When it was all over, Kitten Elizabeth and Wonky Petonky announced, "Josephine! Whoa! That felt good! The water was a little warmer this time, and we didn't need to hide! We feel clean! More! More!"

Emotion coaching (part 2)

"I feel calm!" announced Kitten Elizabeth.

"I feel happy!" added Wonky Petonky.

And so, the three teeth grew to love toothbrushing time. Finally, the toothbrush was their friend.

The End.

Resistance to Change / Trouble with Transitions: Horace the Rock

This story can be told to address a recurring problem or in anticipation of a child having trouble with an upcoming transition. You can also use it as a reminder in an in-the-moment situation.

Introduction

Horace the Rock lived in the forest with his family. Horace was very typical in that he did *not* like to move. He was already good at so many things: sitting still, thinking deep thoughts under the night sky, and, occasionally, being perched upon. Being completely still was his greatest strength.

"Time for lunch!" he'd hear his mama call from the kitchen.

Nope.

"Want to go play outside?" his sister would ask.

No way. Right here is best, he'd think.

"A rolling stone gathers no moss!" his daddy called to him. That's an old rock expression that means if he moved around and tried something new, he'd never get bored. However, being bored sounded perfectly delightful to Horace.

Problem concept

One day, however, Horace got hungry. "I want to get up and get some food, but honestly, I'm not sure how to do it," he announced to no one in particular.

Emotion coaching (part 1)

The more he thought about wanting to move, the sadder he became. He realized that he was missing out on things by being so still all the time. Things like food. Things like play. Things like fun. Maybe sitting still wasn't all it was cracked up to be.

"This sad feeling I have is kind of . . . lonely. Plus, I'm hungry, so as much as I *like* being still, I think I must move. But . . . I'm a little scared of trying since I've never done it before. Transitions are hard."

Resolution

He paused and thought about it. His tummy growled.

I might feel scared, but where there's a will, there's a way! he realized. That's another old rock expression that means we can do something—even something hard—when we decide we want to do it badly enough.

So, using all his strength, he started to sway back and forth a little. The more he rocked, the easier the rocking got. He pushed. He pulled. He tried to make his body as big as it could possibly get.

And suddenly, he burst free! He looked around, bewildered. He looked down and realized he hadn't been a rock at all. He'd *hatched* from an egg! And now, he was a big, beautiful owl!

Well, for now, he was still a little baby owl. But he had wings all the same—and legs, too! He wobbled around a little as he tried to stand, and he felt a freedom he'd never known before.

Where he thought he'd been a rock, he now saw little fragments of broken shell all around him.

His mama smiled down at him. "Time for lunch!" she announced.

"Yes!"

"Want to go play outside?" his sister asked.

"Yes!"

"A rolling stone gathers no moss!" called his daddy.

"And I'm not a stone or a rock at all," Horace replied exuberantly.

Emotion coaching (part 2)

"What a surprise that was!" he announced to his family. "All this time, I thought it was better to be still and stay right where I was. Once I decided to move, though, look what I found! I found all of you! I feel brave and strong! Woohoo! I can't be still forever!"

"There's a time and a place to be still," his mama explained. "You grew well in there. Change and transitions can be hard work. When you decided it was time for something more, though, look at all the joy you found. You just had to be ready—and brave enough to try. Change can be a very good thing."

He nuzzled his mama, and before he knew it, they were all sitting down to a wonderful lunch together. He knew that the next time someone asked him to try something new—to move out of his comfort zone—he'd trust that it would be worth the effort. Smiling to himself, he patted his full tummy and gazed up at the beautiful night sky. He could see it more clearly than ever before.

The End.

Anxiety: Kittenpants, the Barn Kitten

This story can be told to address a recurring problem or in anticipation of a child having trouble with an upcoming social situation. You can also use it as a reminder in an in-the-moment situation.

Note: Why a kitten? Kittens are often perceived, by children and adults alike, as innocent and playful, as well as completely nonthreatening. Other "passive" and small animals may include bunnies and other similar creatures. As such, if the child is feeling "small" like a kitten, they may identify with it well. If your child is a fan of puppies or something else and their barking isn't intimidating to the child, feel free to replace it!

Introduction

Once upon a time, a soft white kitten named Kittenpants lived happily in a barn with her mommy, daddy, and lots of brothers. Every morning, she enjoyed chasing her own tail and pretending to attack the pieces of hay that stuck out from the horses' stalls. She never wandered far from the barn. It was her happy place.

So, in the barn she stayed, happy, warm, and snuggly.

Problem concept

One day, however, her parents told her that the field outside was full of mice, long grass to hide and play in, and lots of butterflies to chase. They announced that they'd be going out together as a family that morning—out of the barn where she felt so comfortable and safe. Kittenpants didn't want to go.

Emotion coaching (part 1)

She felt scared that the wind might blow too hard or that a bird might chirp and startle her. Plus, she worried that her soft white fur might get dirty in the grass and mud puddles she saw outside the barn door. Not to mention, there were other animals out there! The cows were huge compared to her. She felt very, very small and afraid. She did not like feeling out of control, like something terrible might happen.

Seeing that her parents and brothers were getting ready to go, however, she realized that she didn't have much of an option.

Still, she asked, "Daddy? Can we please stay home? I feel scared."

It's always good to talk to an adult about your feelings, you know.

Daddy replied gently, "Kittenpants, I hear that you're afraid. It's normal to feel scared when trying something new. I also know that when you're attacking the pieces of hay in the barn, you can be quite ferocious and brave. I wonder if you remember what that feels like."

Resolution

"Yes, Daddy," Kittenpants answered. "When I'm attacking the hay, I feel very brave. I know I can catch it and pounce on it. I like that feeling."

Just then, she glanced outside and saw a blade of grass just on the other side of the barn door. It was swishing in the wind and looking very much like the pieces of hay that she knew so well.

She realized that if she could pounce on *just that one* blade of grass, she could feel brave outside the barn. She wouldn't have to go any farther.

So, being her most ferocious self, she crouched down, wiggled her hips, twitched her tail—and pounced! She got it!

Much to her surprise, the sun felt warm and nice on her soft white fur.

She saw another blade of grass and decided to pounce on it, too. On through the field she pounced, one tall blade of grass at a time.

She was having so much fun that she didn't even notice when her soft white fur got some mud on it.

And those gigantic cows? Well, they kept to themselves. They barely even noticed her. Kittenpants decided they were just like really big, and really slow, cats. She even imagined they were purring and kneading the field with gigantic paws.

Before she knew it, she was pouncing, leaping, and rolling around in the field, soaking up the sunshine and loving every minute of it.

Emotion coaching (part 2)

Pausing to look up for a moment, she saw her daddy lounging in the sunshine and smiling at her.

"I did it, Daddy! I feel so happy that I made a brave choice! It's fun to be out here, all safe and warm in the sunshine. All I needed to do was remember a part of myself that's ferocious, and then I learned that I can always remember that part of me when something feels scary. I'm so proud of myself!"

And with that, a little yellow butterfly fluttered down and landed right on her nose.

The End.

Bedtime Struggles and Defiance: The Squirrel Whose Ears Fell Off at Bedtime

This story can be told to address a recurring problem. You can also use it as a reminder in an in-the-moment situation.

Introduction and problem concept (Combined)

Sydney Squirrel did not like bedtime. And she *liked* not liking bedtime. After all, her bed had no nuts to bury. Her bed had no other squirrels to chase. Perhaps worst of all, her bed had no chocolate chip cookies in it.

So, every night when Granddad Squirrel told her it was time for bed, do you know what she did?

She hid.

Where did she hide?

Well, she hid under her covers. Her bedcovers. Although it was her bed, it also happened to be the best hiding place in her tree, so she went with it.

Emotion coaching (part 1)

Granddad Squirrel knew where she was hiding, of course. After all, when you find a squirrel hiding under the covers once, it's pretty easy to keep checking there and finding the same squirrel.

He'd amble his way into Sydney Squirrel's bedroom and ask, "Sydney, are you in here?"

(He knew she was in there.)

Every night, she'd respond, "I can't hear you, Granddad. My ears have fallen off, so I don't know that you're telling me it's bedtime."

"Want to come out and talk about it?" he'd ask.

"Sure!" she'd exclaim, excited that she could talk to him instead of staying there in bed. Out from under her covers she'd scamper, ears and all.

One night, they sat down for a snack of applesauce together, as was their nightly ritual. Then, she brushed her teeth, lay down across his lap, and moaned, "I don't want to go to bed, Granddad! I feel sad when it's time to end the day. I'd rather stay up playing with you. Besides, my bed has no nuts, no other squirrels to chase, and no chocolate chip cookies whatsoever."

Resolution

"I hear you're feeling sad about bedtime, Sydney," Granddad responded with empathy. "And I'd like to talk to you about this problem you keep having with your ears falling off. It seems to be a struggle every night. Do we need some ear glue?"

He lovingly reached over and pretended to glue her ears on and secure them to her fuzzy little head. She giggled. "There's no such thing as ear glue, Granddad." Then she added, "But that feels kind of good. Can you keep doing it?"

He replied, "Yes, of course I can. How about if I rub your ears while you start to fall asleep? That'll make sure they stay on tonight."

Emotion coaching (part 2)

Looking forward to the extra affection, she joyfully bounded back into her bedroom and under her covers. Granddad stayed next to her and gently rubbed her ears until she felt nice and relaxed. Just when she was about to fall asleep, she smiled up at him and said, "You know what, Granddad? A little extra love from you helps my ears stay on. I feel peaceful. My ears are tired now. You can go. I love you."

Before he went, he leaned over to the fuzzy ear he'd been rubbing and whispered, "I love you, too. And just so you know, I needed help keeping my ears on when I was your age. Sweet dreams."

The End.

Greediness: The Land of Most

This story can be told to address a recurring problem or in anticipation of a child having trouble with an upcoming situation. You can also use it as a reminder in an in-the-moment situation.

Introduction

Once upon a time, a dragon named Weeble Wobble Wong lived in a far-off land many hundreds of miles from here, and even many hundreds of miles farther than that, in the Land of Most. He was your ordinary, run-of-the-mill purple dragon that plays the ukulele, like all dragons do, as everyone knows.

And also like all other dragons, Weeble Wobble Wong *loved* candy. In fact, that's why most dragons are purple. They eat so much purple candy from the purple candy trees that, well, naturally, they turn purple within their first year of life.

Weeble Wobble Wong loved his life and was always willing to share his purple candy because there was plenty to go around. He never needed to have the most in the Land of Most.

Problem concept

One day, however, Weeble Wobble Wong woke up on the wrong side of the bed. That's dragon language for waking up a little bit grouchy. And on that day, he decided he didn't want to share. He was *sure* that only yesterday, he'd seen his friend Chester Buttercup with an extra piece.

Weeble Wobble Wong vowed to get back at Chester Buttercup. He would sneak over to Chester Buttercup's stash of purple candy from the purple candy tree and take all the biggest pieces for himself. Then, *he'd* have the most!

He'd still leave some purple candy for Chester Buttercup, of course, because he wasn't unreasonable, after all. He'd just make sure that he—himself, the one and only Weeble Wobble Wong—would get the *biggest* pieces. He decided that would be fair enough.

Emotion coaching (part 1)

"I feel so mad!" Weeble Wobble Wong said under his dragon breath. "I don't know for sure that Chester Buttercup had an extra piece, but what if he did? Grrrr. That would make me so angry!"

So, he stomped around, as dragons stomp, playing his angry song on his ukulele. And when he was done, he put down his instrument and tiptoed, as dragons tiptoe, over to Chester Buttercup's part of the kingdom. With him, he carried his smallest pieces of purple candy.

Resolution

As Weeble Wobble Wong approached Chester Buttercup's part of the kingdom, he saw Chester awake and already reaching for the biggest purple candy growing from his purple candy tree.

"I *knew* he never gives me the biggest pieces of candy!" Weeble Wobble Wong seethed. All of a sudden, however, Chester Buttercup turned and saw him.

Weeble Wobble Wong froze. He looked at Chester Buttercup's kind eyes and his outstretched hand, offering him the very same *big* piece of purple candy that he'd just plucked from his purple candy tree.

Weeble Wobble Wong felt his dragon heart soften a bit. He remembered how on his birthday last year, Chester Buttercup had given him an entire dragon-basket *full* of big purple candy. He'd saved it up especially for him.

Suddenly, Weeble Wobble Wong realized he might have been wrong. He dropped the small purple candies and ran to his friend.

"What's going on?" inquired Chester Buttercup.

Emotion coaching (part 2)

"I made a mistake, Chester," Weeble Wobble Wong announced. "You're so generous with me, and I woke up thinking you hadn't been. And even if you did get an extra piece of purple candy yesterday, I know you deserve to have good things, too."

"I still don't know exactly what happened, Weeble Wobble Wong," Chester replied, "but I know you're my friend, and I care about you."

Weeble Wobble Wong continued, "I feel happy that we're friends, and I feel relieved that I was able to see all the ways you're kind to me. It's not about who has the most purple candy. Some days, I have more than you do. Some days, you have more than I do. It all evens out in the end. What matters most is that we care about each other. We always have enough of everything that way."

The two friends sat down together, backs leaned up against each other, and ate their purple candy peacefully, chatting about dragon things. It didn't matter who had more purple candy. Their bellies were full. Even better, their hearts were full of the special love of friendship.

As everyone knows, the Land of Most isn't about how much candy dragons have but about how much goodness they're able to share. It's about who loves the most and who gives the most. Because when everyone gives the most, they all *receive* the most, too.

The End.

Aggression: Herbert Hedgehog and Percy Porcupine

This story can be told to address a recurring problem or in anticipation of a child having trouble with an upcoming social situation. You can also use it as a reminder in an in-the-moment situation.

Introduction

Once upon a time, there were two friends who liked each other so much that they felt like brothers. Herbert Hedgehog and Percy Porcupine spent their days playing together, chasing the forest bugs, and seeing who could fit into the smallest fallen logs on the forest floor.

Problem concept

One day, however, there was a problem. Percy Porcupine had been certain that he could fit into a small hollow log down near the creek, but little did he realize that he'd grown a bit the night before. He found himself suddenly stuck, with his head and front paws snugly inside the log and his backside sticking right out.

Herbert Hedgehog thought he looked incredibly funny, his quilly bottom wiggling back and forth as he tried to pull free. After a while, though, he realized that he needed to help his friend, lest they be stuck there all day. And maybe forever.

So, Herbert Hedgehog went to give his friend Percy Porcupine a big pull. Just as he did, though, Percy yelled, "Hey, who's touching me?" And he poked Herbert Hedgehog right in the nose with one of his sharp quills.

Emotion coaching (part 1)

"Hey! Ouch! That made me mad!" exclaimed Herbert Hedgehog. "I was just trying to help, and you poke me?" Grrrrrr, he felt so angry. And with that, he kicked his friend in the bottom, lodging him even farther into the hollow log.

"Aaaaah!" yelled Percy Porcupine. "You started it!"

"No, you did!" retorted Herbert Hedgehog. Suddenly, the two best friends felt like enemies. They both felt angry.

Resolution

"And what did you mean, 'Who's touching me?'" inquired Herbert Hedgehog. "I was!"

"Oh . . . uh . . . uh-oh," responded Percy Porcupine as he finally wriggled his way free. "I couldn't see anything in there and started to feel scared, so I . . . uh . . . had a big reaction before pausing to think about it."

"Yeah, well, it hurt," replied Herbert Hedgehog. "But you felt scared? I didn't know that. I can see how my kicking you would not make anything better. I had a big reaction without pausing to think about it. I am sorry."

"Me, too," said Percy Porcupine. "Next time, I won't fight back so quickly. I'll stop to check in with myself and see what I'm feeling before I hurt somebody. Even if I'm mad or scared, hurting someone is never the right thing to do. I will slow down and take some deep breaths."

Emotion coaching (part 2)

"Thanks, friend. I think we have a better plan now. I forgive you. Now, race you to the creek!" Herbert Hedgehog raced through the hollow log as if it were a tunnel and splashed his front toes into the water, joyfully.

Meanwhile, Percy Porcupine tried to follow him through the same hollow log and . . . you know what happened next!

The End.

Pestering: Harriet Hucklebee and the Peck Peck Pecking

This story can be told to address a recurring problem or in anticipation of a child having trouble with an upcoming social situation. You can also use it as a reminder in an in-the-moment situation.

Introduction

Once upon a time, a lovely redheaded woodpecker named Harriet Hucklebee lived among the treetops in the Very Tall Forest. She loved gliding among the branches and flying so high she could almost touch the clouds.

Harriet Hucklebee, like many redheaded woodpeckers, is what some would call *persistent*. She knew that the very best way to find her morning breakfast was to peck as fast and as hard as she could at the tree bark. Her persistence nearly always resulted in a tasty meal.

Problem concept

The trouble was, however, that Harriet Hucklebee took the very same approach when she wanted something from one of her friends. One day, for example, she saw her friend Robin Robin with Willy Warbler playing acorn football down near the forest floor. She wanted to join them. So, down she swooped.

In her woodpeckerish way, she didn't just ask one time, "May I play?" Her approach sounded more like:

"I want to play."

"Let me play."

"Can I play?"

And . . .

"Let me play."

"It's my turn."

"Play, play, play!"

To her friends, it sounded like, "Peck, peck, peck, peck, peck, peck, peck . . ." On she continued, hardly taking a breath. Her nonstop pressing felt fairly tiresome for her friends. So, off they flew!

Emotion coaching (part 1)

"Oh, dear!" exclaimed Harriet Hucklebee. "I feel sad and lonely without my friends here. I guess they didn't want to play with me. I wonder why."

All day long, she thought about what happened. She knew how much she wanted to play and how natural it felt to just keep asking and asking and asking . . . but she also observed that asking so many times didn't work at all. In fact, it seemed to make her friends want space from her.

Resolution

The next morning, Harriet Hucklebee woke up and thought, *I still want to play with my friends today. Today, though, I'm going to pay attention to their faces to see if I can figure out how they're feeling before I ask so many times. Maybe my friends need some space sometimes.*

Sure enough, as they usually did, Robin Robin and Willy Warbler started playing together after breakfast time. Harriet Hucklebee observed them from the branch of a nearby tree. It looked like they were having fun together.

"Remember to study their faces," Harriet reminded herself. "I'll see if I can figure out how they're feeling."

Down she swooped and landed next to their playing field. Harriet observed that when they saw her land, their faces looked a little concerned. They started to back up a bit. It didn't look like they wanted to play with her.

Before they could fly away, she said, "Please wait. I apologize for asking so many times yesterday if I could play with you. I know you usually like me, but I can see how you might've felt overwhelmed by all my words. Was that it? I wasn't even giving you a chance to answer. I'd like to try again."

"Yes," offered Robin Robin. "When you keep asking and asking and asking for the same thing, it *does* feel overwhelming and makes us want some space. We value your friendship, though, and we want to play with you—if we can all feel good about it."

Harriet Hucklebee smiled. "In that case, I'll ask just once today, and I'll respect whatever you say. I know your feelings are important, too. May I please join your game?"

Willy Warbler and Robin Robin both flew right over to her and embraced her in their wings.

"Yes," they announced together. "Let's play together! Last one to that tree is a rotten egg!" (That's an old bird joke.)

Emotion coaching (part 2)

"Hooray!" Harriet Hucklebee cried. "I feel so happy to be playing with my friends and so relieved I learned there's a better way to approach them. Pecking and pecking and pecking might work when I'm looking for food, but with friends, I can ask just *once* and know that I've made my point."

And off the three friends flew on the greatest game of chase you've ever seen. They flew so high that they nearly touched the clouds, and Harriet Hucklebee felt so happy that her feelings soared joyfully along with her wings.

The End.

Tidying Up: The Secret Life of the Wooden Toys

This story can be told to address a recurring problem. You can also use it as a reminder in an in-the-moment situation.

Note: I'll preface this by saying I do not believe it is solely a child's responsibility to put away all their toys. I view it as a collaborative effort and a lesson best learned by modeling cooperation and using tools to add joy, such as playful parenting, to otherwise mundane daily tasks.

Introduction

Once upon a time, there was a beautiful wooden box, in a beautiful wooden room, full of beautiful wooden toys. There were wooden dolls and wooden trucks, wooden tools, and wooden paintbrushes.

Normally, the toys took turns playing with the little boy, who was *not* made of wood. He enjoyed the toys thoroughly. As he'd reach his hand into their beautiful wooden home, a toy would always make his way into it and provide hours of happiness to his day.

The toys liked it this way, taking turns playing with him. It gave the rest of them the chance to relax for a while, since this boy had lots of energy. They loved him dearly and wanted to save their energy for when it was their turn to be with this boy.

Problem concept

One day, however, the toys started to argue among themselves. The truck felt rested enough and was ready to drive. The doll wanted to be the one to drive the truck. The wooden tools were sure the truck needed some repairs, and the wooden paintbrushes were positively sure the truck needed painting.

Emotion coaching (part 1)

So, with the boy's help, they all tumbled onto the floor in a big heap, and with an "Oof!" they all demanded the boy's attention, and the next thing anyone knew, toys were *everywhere*.

"I feel jealous," said the doll. "The boy is driving the truck and I'm just sitting here. It should be my turn, not his."

"We feel disappointed," said the paintbrushes. The boy *had* started painting a picture with us, which was great while it lasted, but then he moved on before he was done! Did he forget we're here?"

And on it went, each toy lamenting and complaining, each feeling more like a tripping hazard than something for joy. They were all jumbled up on the floor with hardly any room to walk around them, and no way for others to see each of them for their own beauty.

Resolution

Hearing the toys' disenchantment, the boy looked around and saw that the floor was, indeed, a mess. How could he know what to play with, with far too much in front of him? They really seemed to need a break.

Fortunately, he knew just what to do.

He washed off the paintbrushes, dried them, and laid them carefully back inside their wooden box. The brushes giggled as he moved their bristles; it kind of tickled!

He laid the tools next to them in a neat row in the wooden box. If nothing was broken, there was nothing to fix!

He drove the truck back over the side of the wooden box and bid it good night. When he wasn't looking, the truck blinked a headlight "good night" to him in return.

As for the doll, it kept him company, content to be in his arms without all the "noise" of a too-busy floor with which to share space.

Emotion coaching (part 2)

The paintbrushes sighed in relief, feeling relaxed. The tools smiled a sleepy smile and relaxed, contentedly, back in their home. The truck revved its engine one final time in the wooden box before shutting down, feeling thankful to be at peace again.

The doll, still in the boy's arms, smiled up lovingly at the boy, happily gazing into his eyes as he read her a nighttime story.

As for the boy, he didn't quite know why, but he loved how peaceful and calm everything felt in his beautiful, clean wooden room with the wooden toy box. Likewise, the toys all exhaled peacefully and drifted off to sleep.

The End.

Fears: The Darkness Who Was Afraid of the Boy

This story can be told to address a recurring problem. You can also use it as a reminder in an in-the-moment situation.

Introduction

Once upon a time, the Darkness had a great big problem. You see, she loved being alone; she yearned to feel peaceful and calm without any of the noise and energy of Light.

"Oof. Who'd want all that energy of Daytime and Light?" Darkness wondered. "In the Light, you can see so many things to be *afraid* of! It's much safer to be Darkness. Safe, safe Darkness. Peaceful Darkness. Nothing to see. Nothing to fear. I am so very safe."

She took some deep, calming breaths to get the images of Light out of her mind.

Problem concept

In fact, Darkness believed she had a very good reason to be afraid of Light. You see, every night, just as Darkness was ready to go to sleep, someone flipped a switch and poured Light into the room.

How jolting!

How unnerving!

How wrong!

To make things worse—as if the Light weren't terrifying enough—every night, a little boy bounded into the room along with the Light. Darkness heard far-off voices call it *bedtime*, but who could sleep with this boy invading the Darkness?

Even worse, the boy brought wiggles into the room!

And laughter!

And—gasp—bounces on the bed!

Finally, the boy would scamper under the covers and lie there, still wiggling, until he finally fell asleep.

Emotion coaching (part 1)

Darkness didn't like wiggles, laughter, or bounces one bit. They were far too wiggly, and noisy, and bouncy, and totally unpredictable!

How could Darkness sleep, wondering every night when this was going to happen? It was so disruptive!

"I feel emotionally exhausted," confessed Darkness to herself. "I'm terrified of being terrified. And I'm downright tired of being terrified." With that, Darkness shut her eyes as tightly as she could and covered her ears.

Resolution

After 52 wiggles, 87 laughs, and 4,832,649 bounces on the bed, Darkness realized that living in fear was useless. She really was tired of feeling tired and tired of worrying.

Fear certainly wasn't getting less terrifying—and being terrified just seemed to grow the fear. Something had to change.

So, Darkness started by drawing a picture of Light. Somehow drawing a picture of it, and being in control of it, made Darkness feel a little safer imagining it. After a while, Darkness drew some of the other objects that are visible in the Light, including the boy's bed.

Darkness wasn't ready to draw the boy yet, though. That felt too scary. (After all, the boy had wiggles.)

After a few more sleepless nights, Darkness decided to draw the boy's teddy bear. Then his legs—but only his legs.

Finally, feeling that Darkness would never feel comfortable drawing the boy's body and face, Darkness drew a picture of a pink balloon (instead of a head) on top of the boy's legs.

That made Darkness laugh, so Darkness added a fancy hat with lots of purple and green feathers on it. Instead of arms, Darkness imagined the boy had two fluffy pillows at his sides and couldn't pick anything up. Darkness started imagining the boy's name was Balloon Head, and that made Darkness laugh more.

Emotion coaching (part 2)

Eventually, the whole picture Darkness had drawn looked so very silly that it was nearly impossible to be afraid of the Light. In fact, Darkness said, "Oh my goodness! I've made such a silly picture that now I actually want more Light so I can see more ideas for more silly things to draw! I'm not even scared anymore!"

And to herself, Darkness added, "Come in, Balloon Head. I can't wait to feel your silly wiggles tonight! Wow, I think I'm actually excited about this."

With that, Darkness realized that she was no longer afraid of the Light. Or the boy. Or his 5,987 wiggles or his 8,924,012 laughs, or even his 200 bazillion bounces on the bed. In fact, Darkness welcomed them and fell peacefully asleep each night, feeling great comfort and safety.

The End.

Toilet Learning: Bouncy Bunny's Litter Box

This story can be told proactively or to address a recurring problem. You can also use it as a reminder in an in-the-moment situation.

Introduction

Bouncy Bunny was a beautiful little rabbit. She was brave and kind and loved to try new things like the slide at the playground, the swings, and yummy new garden treats.

Well, she liked trying *almost* all new things. Sometimes she didn't like trying carrots that had bends in them or lettuce that had been walked on by the local deer. Mostly, though, she liked new things. She was brave that way.

Problem concept

One day, however, a strange box showed up in her den. Mama explained that it was called a *litter box*, and she told her how it worked.

Emotion coaching (part 1)

Bouncy Bunny thought it sounded great! She agreed it was perfect . . . for the *other* bunnies. Not for her, though. No, no, not for her. She liked things just the way they were.

Her mama patted her little bunny head and gave her a kiss. Mama then asked her how it made her feel to see the litter box in their den.

"Just no," replied Bouncy Bunny. "I don't like it."

Mama looked at her tenderly and said, "I wonder if it makes you feel nervous."

Bouncy Bunny nodded. New things—*some* new things, anyway—made her feel nervous.

Resolution

"I understand," replied Mama. "You know what? You don't have to use it until you're ready. I believe in you, and I trust that you'll soon feel good about it." And for the next few months, Mama simply invited Bouncy Bunny to sit near the litter box and observe while Mama used it herself. No pressure. No pushing.

Mama waited. Mama trusted.

Bouncy Bunny kept watching.

One day in early spring, Mama noticed that Bouncy Bunny was sniffing around near the litter box. Mama hopped over, kissed Bouncy Bunny on her left ear, and said nothing (even though she really wanted to say something).

Looking into Mama's eyes, Bouncy Bunny quietly asked, "May I try it?"

Giving her another quick kiss on her right ear this time, Mama gently and lovingly lifted Bouncy Bunny into the litter box, making sure to keep a loving paw on her shoulder the whole time.

Emotion coaching (part 2)

Bouncy Bunny's eyes got wide. She looked at Mama and asked, "Did I do it?"

Mama nodded proudly.

"I feel so brave," announced Bouncy Bunny. "So proud of myself!"

"I'm proud of you, too, Bouncy Bunny." Mama smiled, and out of the den they hopped on to a wonderful new adventure.

The End.

Handling Disappointment: Adventure Jimmy and the Red Cup

This story can be told to address a recurring problem or in anticipation of a child having trouble with an upcoming situation. You can also use it as a reminder in an in-the-moment situation.

Parenting note: As a general rule, when a child has a big emotional release about something like the color of the cup they receive, the stress they exhibit is rarely about the color of the cup. This is usually the scapegoat for some bigger stress that they've been carrying, and it manifests as stress around what we consider to be trivial things. It helps to reframe these incidents as the proverbial straw that broke the camel's back and examine the stress behind the emotional release.

Introduction

Once upon a time, Adventure Jimmy woke up and knew *just* what he'd do that day. He'd have his breakfast in his blue bowl, drink his water from his red cup, go put on his cape, and then go play with his favorite toy rocket ship. He couldn't wait! Everything was perfect in his mind.

Problem concept

When he sat down to breakfast, however, he saw that Mommy had put his blue cup in front of him. His plan was ruined! He didn't want the blue cup; he wanted the red one! No other cup would do.

His lip started to tremble, and he announced, "I want my red cup."

"Sorry, sweetheart, it's in the dishwasher."

Emotion coaching (part 1)

With that, Adventure Jimmy got so mad that he pushed his entire bowl of cereal onto the floor and made a big mess. He hadn't meant to do that. It just kind of happened in his anger. Now he felt overwhelmed, too. Even worse, now his dog was starting to lap up his breakfast from the floor. He started to yell and cry.

Resolution

Mommy shooed away the dog, put a towel over the mess, and pulled Adventure Jimmy onto her lap.

"You seem really upset," she said. "Let's take some big bubble breaths together."

Once Adventure Jimmy calmed down, she added, "I wonder what's going on for you."

He told her everything about his foiled plan. When he was done, he asked, "Why is my red cup in the dishwasher, Mama? I need it!"

She told him that it was dirty. He paused, thinking.

"Wait. If it's dirty, why don't we just take it out and you can wash it? You can use the soap and the sponge!"

She paused, saying that she wasn't planning to hand wash more dishes that morning.

After a moment of feeling disappointed, Adventure Jimmy perked up, saying, "I'll do it! Will you show me how?"

She agreed that was reasonable. She invited Adventure Jimmy to help wipe up the big spill from the floor, and once that was done, they went to the sink together.

Adventure Jimmy scrubbed his red cup until it was perfectly clean.

Emotion coaching (part 2)

"I did it! I solved the problem!"

Together, they filled his cup.

"I'm so happy, Mama. I have my cup, *and* I learned how to wash dishes! Can I do all the dishes from now on?"

She raised her eyebrows and agreed that he could definitely help with the dishes from now on. It could be his new special helper plan. Smiling, they enjoyed their perfect breakfast together.

The End.

Emotional Intelligence and Empathy: Ulysses Unicorn and The Feeling-Seeing Glasses

This story can be told to address a recurring problem or in anticipation of a child having trouble with an upcoming situation. You can also use it as a reminder in an in-the-moment situation.

Introduction

Ulysses the Unicorn had a special power. I'm not talking about your everyday-ordinary unicorn powers of healing the other forest creatures with his horn, and flying, and all that other ho-hum standard stuff. I mean a very, very, *very* special power.

He could see people's feelings. He could tell when they were feeling sad or excited or angry or happy or even if they simply had too many wiggles trapped inside that they wanted to get out. He had a special name for his superpower. He called it *empathy*. But because that's kind of a big word, most of his friends just called it his Feeling-Seeing power.

Problem concept

The problem was, however, his Feeling-Seeing power only worked when he sat down, observed the animal friend whose feelings he wanted to see, and put on his magical Feeling-Seeing glasses.

If he forgot those glasses, he had nothing. No skill. No power. No seeing of anyone's feelings.

One day, when he was bounding through the forest, he leaped right over Frances Fish swimming along in her stream. He heard her making a soft sound and saw water dripping down from her eyes.

Emotion coaching (part 1)

"Oh, dear," Ulysses the Unicorn said. "What's the matter? I didn't bring my Feeling-Seeing glasses so I have no way to understand, and now I feel worried! How can I help? What shall I do if I can't see your feelings?"

Resolution

Frances Fish blinked up at him from under the water and said, "Here, take these."

She handed him a pair of invisible nothings.

"What are these?" inquired a perplexed Ulysses.

"They're invisible Feeling-Seeing glasses. If you put them on, I think they'll work."

Sure enough, when Ulysses the Unicorn put them on and sat down on a rock beside her stream, he realized that he could see more than he'd originally thought. He looked around and noticed that she was alone without her sisters and brothers.

"I think I understand," Ulysses said. "I see that the water running down your face might be tears, and tears sometimes mean you're sad. I also see that your siblings are up the stream a bit, playing without you, so I wonder if you're lonely."

"Yes!" responded Frances Fish. "Well, I *was* lonely, anyway. I wanted a break from all their activity, but I didn't want to be alone, either. Now that you're here, my loneliness is gone, and my tears are drying up!"

"Drying up in the stream?" Ulysses asked.

They both laughed.

"Now I see you're laughing," Ulysses observed. "That must mean you're feeling happy again."

Emotion coaching (part 2)

"Wait—hold on!" he continued. "How did I see how you felt without my usual magical glasses?"

Wise little Frances Fish explained, "It's because you never saw feelings with your eyes in the first place. You see them with your heart every time you slow down and observe someone else's experience. You watch their face to see what they're feeling, and then you can make guesses about what's going on. In a way, you allow yourself to feel *their* feelings, even though you know they're separate from your own."

Ulysses exclaimed, "Amazing! You mean I've had this superpower all along? All I have to do is slow down long enough and observe someone else to see what they're feeling? My Feeling-Seeing power comes from within me? I'm going to practice this all day!"

He gently patted his little friend's head and scampered off while Frances Fish swam happily back to her family. Ulysses spent the rest of the day watching his animal friends' faces, noticing how they were feeling, and making sure he always kept his invisible Feeling-Seeing glasses handy.

The End.

Part 7:

USING "YES, AND . . ." IMPROV COMEDY, FINAL THOUGHTS, AND THE NOT-END OF THIS BOOK

Have you ever read a story that simply doesn't leave you after you've closed the book? I've got a few of those (most recently, it was the *Anne of Green Gables* series, which I somehow missed until just last year).

Stories stick with us because they're teachers. The characters reflect parts of our inner selves—the parts we show to others as well as the deep, dark corners that few know about. We resonate with the characters because they *are* us. They validate us and give us new perspectives. They give us a *yes* to everything we're thinking and feeling, showing us on paper that we're normal.

Interestingly, the concept of "Yes, and . . ." is one of the cornerstones of improv comedy. In short, it means that when comedians are supporting one another onstage, they never negate the storyline that someone else has initiated.

For example, if I come onstage pretending to be a cow, more than likely, someone is going to hand me some imaginary grass to chew on or try to milk me. (Yikes!) My "reality" is what they work with, and they may even join me in the pasture.

Not only does this level of support entertain the audience, but it also creates an incredible sense of safety for the performers. They know that whatever they bring is safe there. Their fellow improvisers are going to welcome it and build onto it however they can.

We can meet our children with this same kind of safety by:

- Validating their feelings rather than dismissing them.
- Seeing how much they want to do the thing they're doing, and finding ways that they can. ("I see how much you want to splash water. Let's go do it in the bath!")
- Showing them through our words and actions that they belong here, just as they are.

When we weave this level of support into our daily lives with our kids—through stories and otherwise—they "feel felt," as Dr. Daniel J. Siegel says. They realize, "Hey, this person really gets me."

Feeling supported in this way helps them carry their inner stories forward—the ones they've heard, as well as the stories they believe to be true about themselves.

When those stories are affirming, validating, and loving, they never really end. They become the stories that help heal the world one child at a time.

Part 8:

RESOURCES AND REFERENCES

I encourage you to read the Covenant for Honouring Children available at the Raffi Foundation for Child Honouring, and to take the course if it speaks to your heart. I know it spoke to mine. This is a short excerpt:

> The Covenant . . . is a promise to love, respect and be kind to children. . . . The embodiment of life, liberty and happiness, children are original blessings, here to learn their own song. Every child is entitled to love, to dream and belong to a loving 'village.' And to pursue a life of purpose.

Conscious Parenting is one of nine principles of Child Honouring. Learn more at https://www.raffifoundation.org/child/the-covenant/.

Authors I Enjoy

All of these authors have helped me improve my own parenting journey, so I want to share their gifts with you as well. Please check my website at https://www.dandelion-seeds.com for a complete list of resources I trust. This list is just the beginning, and it's ever evolving.

Jessica Joelle Alexander
Dr. Nicole Beurkens
Dr. Michele Borba
Drs. Robert Brooks and Samuel Goldstein
Tina Payne Bryson, PhD
Jamie Chaves, OTD, OTR/L
Iris Chen
Dr. Lawrence J. Cohen
Stephen Cosgrove
Jenn Curtis, MSW
Dr. Mona Delahooke
Rebecca Eanes
Phyllis Fagell, LCPC
Dr. Peter Gray
Ross Greene, PhD
Devorah Heitner
Ned Johnson
Jessica Lahey
Dr. Anne Lane
Janet Lansbury
Dr. Vanessa Lapointe
Katherine Reynolds Lewis
Julie Lythcott-Haims
Deborah MacNamara, PhD
Dr. Laura Markham
Dr. Gabor Maté
Audrey Monke
Cynthia Clumeck Muchnick, MA
Dr. Jane Nelsen

Dr. Gordon Neufeld
Andrew Newman
Dr. Meghan Owenz
Elizabeth Pantley
Annie Murphy Paul
Kim John Payne, MEd
Debbie Reber
Bethany Saltman
Daniel J. Siegel, MD
Dr. William Stixrud
Tessa Stuckey
Dr. Ashley Taylor

Acknowledgments

To my daughter. I love you to the edge of the universe and back. I'm very proud of you, and I like you just the way you are. *Je t'aime, ma fée.*

To Andy, my brother from another mother, for encouraging me to keep writing way back when. You were the first one to make putting my heart on paper feel really, truly safe (aside from the times that it still feels terrifying, but your voice is there in these moments, too).

To little Pablo, because you always deserved kindness.

To Shelley, for your steadfast and unwavering friendship; to Kristy, my beloved bad influence, for gallivanting around the globe with me and helping me decide on the "R"; to Laryngectomy, my very first friend who's loved me always and will forever meet me at the Terrace and go see the animals with me; and of course, to Mike, whom I've married repeatedly.

To my identical cousin, for being the best Fairy Godmother, and her family—our family—for all those years of preserving the immortal tarantula bows.

To my mom, for being a cycle breaker.

To Sonja and Pastor Greg, who started me down my right path. Thanks to you, I know peace.

To my daughter in Heaven. Thanks, God, for taking care of her for me (and for taking care of the rest of us, too).

To Tommy, my SL, for repeatedly being my personal first responder, and to all the guys in our circle growing up—namely, Paul, Ron, Tom, and Ned (whoa, Nelly!). You were an incredible source of love and safety for me.

To Neil and the PC group, thanks for being my "home" in a place I never intended to land. I write more because of you, and sometimes I write right, right? You were good and safe and healthy for me in all the ways.

To the authors who not only helped guide my own parenting but also embraced me as a friend in this work—thank you.

To all the friends who, in my heart, are my living, loving family.

To my great-granny, Grandma Kiddy, and Granddad; how kind you always were to me and how I miss you. I want to be like you when I grow up.

To Raffi and Luna for bringing out my inner changemaker, for a lovely evening of connection and child-honoring discussion on your porch, and for my daughter's first piano lesson. I moved forward in this work largely because of you.

To ma jumelle, Cathy, et ma famille française.

To all the teachers who encouraged me and fueled my passion for learning.

To Montréal, for opening all the doors for me.

To my editors, Delphine Gatehouse and Kerry Stapley, who magically homed in on exactly the areas of this book that gave me pause and made them feel so much more right, I thank you.

To Tina Brackins, Project Manager extraordinaire, for all your wisdom and guidance.

To Nicole, my selfless and generous illustrator, who helped this book come alive. You're very much a part of this book's soul. It's for kind mamas like you that I'm doing this work in the first place.

To everyone who's shown emotional generosity to another when they didn't have to.

To all those who've shown up for me and allowed me to show up for you.

I love you.

Oh, and to that doctor I mention in the preface—thanks for lighting the fire in my belly. Good news. I've gotten serious about parenting. I now feel incredible gratitude to you.

Additional References

- [1] https://www.npr.org/2019/03/04/689925669/storytelling-instead-of-scolding-inuit-say-it-makes-their-children-more-cool-hea
- https://www.jstor.org/stable/25765124?seq=1
- https://www.nationalgeographic.org/article/storytelling-and-cultural-traditions/
- https://extension.sdstate.edu/why-spending-quality-time-your-children-important
- https://www.researchgate.net/publication/254301584_The_Creativity_Crisis_The_Decrease_in_Creative_Thinking_Scores_on_the_Torrance_Tests_of_Creative_Thinking
- https://www.verywellmind.com/an-overview-of-the-types-of-emotions-4163976
- https://dandelion-seeds.com/positive-parenting/co-regulation/
- https://www.pesi.com/blog/details/959/video-emotional-responsiveness-with-dr-tina-payne-bryson
- https://yourkidstable.com/proprioceptive-activities/
- http://sensory-modulation-brisbane.com/sensory-modulation-blog/balance-and-anxiety
- https://www.health.harvard.edu/blog/ease-anxiety-and-stress-take-a-belly-breather-2019042616521#:~:text=Belly%2obreathing%20stimulates%20the%20vagus,pressure%20and%20lowering%20stress%20levels.

- https://www.ncbi.nlm.nih.gov/pmc/articles/PMC3621648/#:~:text=The%20development%20and%20maturation%20of%20the%20prefrontal%20cortex%20occurs%20primarily,helps%20accomplish%20executive%20brain%20functions.
- https://www.ncbi.nlm.nih.gov/pmc/articles/PMC6456824/
- https://www.ncbi.nlm.nih.gov/pmc/articles/PMC3150158/
- https://www.ncbi.nlm.nih.gov/pmc/articles/PMC6469458/
- https://www.ncbi.nlm.nih.gov/pmc/articles/PMC3939772/
- https://www.zerotothree.org/espanol/brain-development
- https://www.zerotothree.org/resources/2648-who-am-i-developing-a-sense-of-self-and-belonging
- https://www.ncbi.nlm.nih.gov/pmc/articles/PMC4017914/#:~:text=The%20insula%20is%20one%20of,et%20al.%2C%202011%5D.
- https://www.ncbi.nlm.nih.gov/pmc/articles/PMC3019061/
- https://www.ncbi.nlm.nih.gov/pmc/articles/PMC4141473/
- https://link.springer.com/article/10.1007/s40653-020-00307-z
- https://dandelion-seeds.com/positive-parenting/peaceful-parenting/
- https://www.ncbi.nlm.nih.gov/pmc/articles/PMC5681963/
- https://www.health.harvard.edu/staying-healthy/exercising-to-relax#:~:text=Add%20a%20little%20strength%20training,deep%20breathing%20or%20muscular%20relaxation.
- https://www.livesinthebalance.org/kids-do-well-if-they-can

- https://www.science.org.au/curious/people-medicine/how-memory-develops
- Source: https://www.webmd.com/balance/features/is-crying-good-for-you#1
- https://www.ndsu.edu/faculty/pavek/Psych486_686/chapterpdfs1stedKolb/kolb_07.pdf
- https://dandelion-seeds.com/positive-parenting/video-interview-with-dr-ross-greene/
- https://en.wikipedia.org/wiki/Serendipity_(book_series)
- https://study.com/academy/topic/short-behavior-and-feelings-stories-for-kids.html
- https://www.hawthornpress.com/books/storytelling/storytelling-storytelling/healing-stories-for-challenging-behaviour/
- https://www.ncbi.nlm.nih.gov/pmc/articles/PMC3898692/
- https://www.sciencedaily.com/releases/2012/03/120307132206.htm
- https://dandelion-seeds.com/positive-parenting/playful-parenting-2/
- "HUG" process visual my own and generated with Canva

About the Author

Sarah R. Moore is the founder of Dandelion Seeds Positive Parenting, an author, speaker, armchair neuroscientist, and most importantly, a Mama. She's a lifelong learner with training in child development, trauma recovery, interpersonal neurobiology, and improv comedy. As a certified Master Trainer in conscious parenting, she helps bring JOY, EASE, and CONNECTION back to families around the globe. Her work has been featured in HuffPost, Scary Mommy, Motherly, Her View from Home, and The Natural Parent Magazine, among others. Based in Colorado, Sarah and her family spend much of their time worldschooling. (She speaks French and eats Italian food like a pro!) Her heart's desire is to bring greater peace and healing to the world through loving and respectful parenting.

To read Sarah's blog and learn about the services she offers, go to https://www.dandelion-seeds.com or scan this QR code:

To sign up for Sarah's self-paced mini-courses, go to https://dandelion-seeds.com/courses/ or scan this QR code:

Printed in the USA
CPSIA information can be obtained
at www.ICGtesting.com
LVHW021637211223
767154LV00011B/437

9 781643 43675